D1710611

privacy in the
ONLINE WORLD

Online Privacy
and Social Media

Carla Mooney

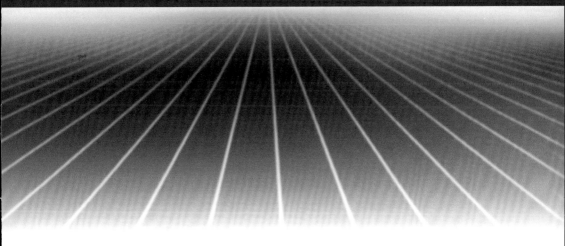

ReferencePoint
Press®

San Diego, CA

DUBOIS

ReferencePoint
Press®

About the Author

Carla Mooney is the author of many books for young adults and children.
She lives in Pittsburgh, Pennsylvania, with her husband and three children.

For more information, contact:
ReferencePoint Press, Inc.
PO Box 27779
San Diego, CA 92198
www. ReferencePointPress.com

Picture Credits
Cover: Thinkstock Images; AP Images: 39, 50; © Simon Chavez/dpa/Corbis: 9; © Jim Craigmyle/Corbis: 14,
20; © Jutta Klee/ableimages/Corbis: 55; © Todd Korol/Reuters/Corbis: 47; © Anupam Nath/AP/Corbis: 43;
© Ron Sachs/CNP/Corbis: 31; © Tan Shung Sin/Reuters/Corbis: 26; © Erik Tham/Corbis: 5; Thinkstock
Images: 35; © Alex Milan Tracy/NurPhoto/Corbis: 61

LIBRARY OF CONGRESS CATALOGING-IN-PUBLICATION DATA

Mooney, Carla, 1970–
  Online privacy and social media / by Carla Mooney.
    pages cm. — (Privacy in the online world)
  Includes bibliographical references and index.
  ISBN-13: 978-1-60152-730-1 (hardback)
  ISBN-10: 1-60152-730-6 (hardback)
  1. Online social networks—Security measures—Juvenile literature. 2. Privacy, Right of—Juvenile
literature. 3. Computer security—Juvenile literature. 4. Social media—Juvenile literature. I. Title.
  HM742.M658 2015
  302.30285—dc23
                                                                            2014012131

Contents

Unintended Consequences

In 2012 Yuri Wright was one of the top high school football prospects in America, playing senior cornerback at Don Bosco Preparatory High School in New Jersey. Several prestigious college football programs were recruiting him. Then in January 2012, Wright was expelled from Don Bosco because of his posts on social media. His dream of a college football scholarship was in jeopardy.

Wright made a mistake common among social media users: He thought his Twitter account, which had sixteen hundred followers, was private. But school officials and college coaches were reading his Twitter feed, which he used to tweet comments that included profanity and racial language and were sometimes sexually explicit. "He was expelled from the school for the things he had written on Twitter," says Greg Toal, Wright's high school football coach. "It was pretty simple really, what he wrote were some graphic sex things. This is a Catholic school, things like that cannot happen. It was totally inappropriate."[1]

According to Toal, the Don Bosco staff repeatedly warned Wright and his teammates about the dangers of social media. "We told them about 10 or 15 times to get off (Twitter) and not to be involved in it, but there is always somebody who thinks he knows better," says Toal. "What he wrote was pretty bad, to be honest with you, I can't even say what he wrote. . . . He was told on numerous occasions not to be Twittering and there are consequences for his actions."[2] After learning about his explicit tweets, the University of Michigan reportedly stopped recruiting Wright and rescinded a scholarship offer. Wright eventually committed to play football at the University of Colorado.

Profanity and sexually explicit talk are not a new phenomenon in teenage locker rooms. Before social media, however, these conversations stayed behind closed doors, heard only by those in the room. The advent of social media has stripped away such privacy. Once something is posted online today, it is out there for anyone to read, forward, and copy.

Preston Wages, a University of Arizona compliance coordinator, understands how social media can damage a person's reputation.

Many social media users, including those who frequent Twitter, mistakenly think that all of their posts are private. Even those who have strong privacy settings are not always protected.

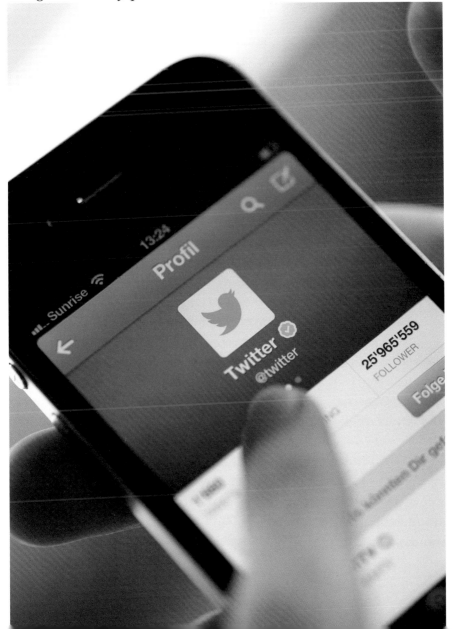

He educates athletes at the University of Arizona about social media and privacy. He warns young people that nothing on the Internet is private forever. As part of his job, Wages monitors athletcs' Twitter feeds and Facebook pages. He is amazed at how much private information is posted online. "Some people use it almost like a text message," says Wages. "They don't think it's public. Their friends aren't the only ones looking at their sites."[3] Even with privacy settings, social media posts are not completely private. Wages says that many young people could easily be tricked into accepting a friend request from a fake profile, letting that person in to read private posts. "All I would really have to do is create some fake Twitter account and then put some hot girl's picture on it and pretend to be somebody else," says Wages. "They'd let me right in."[4]

> "He was expelled from the school for the things he had written on Twitter."[1]
>
> —*Greg Toal, football coach of suspended player Yuri Wright at Don Bosco Preparatory High School.*

Cases like Wright's illustrate the growing conflict between online privacy and social media. Popular social media sites like Facebook, Twitter, Instagram, and YouTube make it easy for people to share their photos, locations, thoughts, and other personal information with friends and acquaintances. Sitting at home, users feel a sense of anonymity and security that may lead them to be freer in what information they post online than what they might reveal in person.

Yet while social media may feel personal and private, it is frequently open for the public to read. In addition, social media companies are collecting user information with every click in order to sell data to advertising networks and other parties. For users, the consequences of private information becoming public can be long-lasting and devastating, no matter how it occurs.

Wright's case serves as a stern warning for social media users: Posts typed in just a few seconds can haunt users for years to come. In Wright's case, even though he has taken down his Twitter feed, numerous screen shots of his offensive tweets are available on sites around the Internet. His words will live on indefinitely, whether he wants them to or not.

Chapter 1

The History of Privacy and Social Media

The concept of privacy has been important to Americans for generations. "Few aspects of personal privacy are more important than the confidentiality of one's thoughts and communications. . . . Human nature being what it is, there are countless reasons why we value the power to choose who, if anyone, hears what we have to say on a particular subject,"[5] writes author and attorney Frederick S. Lane in his book *American Privacy: The 400-Year History of Our Most Contested Right*.

Although privacy is not specifically guaranteed in the US Constitution, most people believe it is addressed in the Fourth Amendment. The amendment states, "The right of the people to be secure in their persons, houses, papers, and effects, against unreasonable searches and seizures, shall not be violated, and no Warrants shall issue, but upon probable cause, supported by Oath or affirmation, and particularly describing the place to be searched, and the persons or things to be seized."[6] Before computers and the Internet, this amendment protected the privacy of citizens. If police officers wanted to gather private details about a person's habits and lifestyle, they had to obtain a search warrant before they could search the person's home or listen to his or her phone calls. To obtain the warrant, police had to convince a judge that they had probable cause, or that they could reasonably expect the search to yield evidence of a crime. These requirements protected Americans from unlawful, random searches.

With widespread use of computers and the Internet, however, the protection of privacy under the Fourth Amendment has become more indistinct. If a person shares information freely with others online, can he or she claim it is private? According to several Supreme Court rulings, the government does not need a search warrant to obtain personal documents if a person has already shared them with someone else online. In the digital age, people reveal many details about their lives on social media, from birthdays and addresses to religious beliefs and political ideals. Suddenly it becomes unclear whether this information is private or public.

Even though the Internet and social media are creating new privacy issues, Americans still strongly support privacy rights and want to have the ability to control the flow of their personal information. Abby Drumm, a twenty-year-old from Indianapolis, says that she has had problems in the past with family members reading social media posts intended for close friends. Since then she says she has taken various steps to hide her online activity so fewer people can see what she posts or find her on social media. According to a study released in 2013 by the Pew Research Center's Internet & American Life Project, 50 percent of Internet users are worried about the information available about them online, while 86 percent have tried to hide their activity online. Some say they are trying to protect themselves from criminals and hackers, while others want to block advertisers or keep certain information out of the hands of family members, spouses, employers, or the government. "These findings reinforce the notion that privacy is not an all-or-nothing proposition for Internet users," says Mary Madden, a senior researcher at Pew. "People choose different strategies for different activities, for different content, to mask themselves from different people, at different times in their lives. What they clearly want is the power to decide who knows what about them."[7]

> "People choose different strategies for different activities, for different content, to mask themselves from different people, at different times in their lives. What they clearly want is the power to decide who knows what about them."[7]
>
> —Mary Madden, a senior researcher at the Pew Research Center.

Advent of Web 2.0

For decades Americans have announced personal details about births, deaths, marriages, and social events in public newspapers. Athletes have reported accomplishments, citizens have talked about community awards, and students have celebrated graduations and honors in the newspaper.

The introduction of the World Wide Web in 1991 provided a new platform for people to share thoughts and information. The web enabled users to create, organize, and link documents and web pages so that other people could easily read them over the Internet. Web browsers provided the software to translate web pages and data into an easy-to-read format on computer screens, allowing people of all ages and backgrounds to easily use the Internet.

At first most web content was created by companies and organizations to provide information about themselves. Around 2002,

With 500 million registered users, YouTube is one of the largest and most popular social media sites. According to one survey, web users spend an average of five hours per week on the site.

The Positives of Social Media

Although news reports about teens and social media often focus on negatives, such as cyberbullying, many teens report participating in social media can be a positive experience. According to a 2012 report by the nonprofit child advocacy group Common Sense Media, 20 percent of teens said social media made them feel more confident, compared to 4 percent who said it made them feel less confident. More than half of the teens surveyed (52 percent) said social media made their relationships with friends better, whereas only 4 percent said it negatively affected those relationships. "On the whole, teens said that they feel that social media has a more positive than negative impact on their social and emotional lives," says Shira Lee Katz, Common Sense Media's director of digital media. "They believe that social media helps their friendships, makes them feel more outgoing and gives them confidence."

Eileen Masio from New York monitors her thirteen-year-old daughter Amelia's Instagram account and says she has seen the positive and supporting interaction between her daughter and her friends on the site. "I think just as damaging as social media can be, it can . . . help to build self-confidence, too," says Masio, "When they post selfies, all the comments I usually see are 'You're beautiful,' 'You're so pretty,' 'Oh my God, gorgeous.'"

Quoted in Kelly Wallace, "The Upside of Selfies: Social Media Isn't All Bad for Kids," CNN, November 22, 2013. www.cnn.com.

however, the way in which people used the Internet and the web began to change. Individual users began to generate and upload their own content onto the web. The term *Web 2.0* was coined to describe the trend of user-generated content. People posted writing, pictures, video, and music. They invited other users to read, view, and comment on their posts, and the web became immensely popular. "The remarkable rise of the World Wide Web was fueled in large part by an apparently insatiable desire on the part of the average person to publicize information about himself or herself on a seemingly endless number of subjects,"[8] writes Lane.

Out of the Web 2.0 world grew social media. Social media are Internet sites that encourage people to interact, share thoughts, and discuss information online. Social media takes many forms, including blogs, forums, message boards, social networks, video and photo sharing sites, and podcasts. These sites use a variety of media, including text, pictures, video, and audio. They allow users to create a list of friends or followers, update their status and post content, comment on other users' statuses and content, and send private messages. Popular social media sites include Facebook, LinkedIn, Twitter, YouTube, Instagram, Pinterest, Blogger, and many others.

Since its introduction, social media has exploded in popularity around the world. According to the Pew Internet & American Life survey, 73 percent of adults used social networking sites as of September 2013. Facebook, Twitter, and YouTube are some of the largest sites, with 1.11 billion, 1 billion, and 500 million registered users, respectively. While online, Americans spend increasing amounts of time on social media, taking advantage of multiple platforms and logging in frequently. According to a 2013 survey of Americans conducted by the Buntin Group and Survey Sampling International, web users spent an average of 6.8 hours per week on Facebook, followed by 5 hours on YouTube and 4.2 hours on Twitter.

Privacy Expectations

While online, users have certain expectations of privacy. They want to browse the Internet, use social media, and post content without anyone tracking their movements. Many have a false sense of security, believing that only friends and other authorized users are viewing their social media updates. When they do provide personal information, users expect that it will be used only in authorized ways. In addition, users expect that social media companies will closely guard their online information and not share personal data with third parties.

What many people do not realize is that these expectations do not match the reality of what is happening online. Many people use social media to interact with friends, unaware of how easily their online interactions can be made public for the world to see. A personal online chat between two friends can be screen shot, uploaded to another site, and shared with a potentially large, unintended audience. When users go online to upload photos, update statuses, or "like" a friend's post, they leave a digital footprint that can be followed for years. Every move a user makes online through computers, smartphones, and tablets can become information that can be collected, stored, and shared. Privacy experts say that users often do not know how quickly they can lose control of information on social media. "Users are often unaware of the extent to which their information is available," says Chris Conley, technology and civil liberties attorney at the American Civil Liberties Union of Northern California. "And if sensitive info is released, it is often impossible to put the cat back in the bag."[9]

> "Users are often unaware of the extent to which their information is available. And if sensitive info is released, it is often impossible to put the cat back in the bag."[9]
>
> —Chris Conley, technology and civil liberties attorney at the American Civil Liberties Union of Northern California.

Growing Privacy Concerns

Once posted on social media, details intended to be private can quickly become exposed for anyone to see, or they may get used in unintended ways. Photos taken at a party, for example, may be viewed by school officials, college recruiters, and potential employers. Personal photos and other details can be copied and used for an unauthorized purpose without notifying the user.

In 2014 blogger Rachele Cateyes discovered that personal photos she had put online were being used without her knowledge or consent for a cause she did not support. As an advocate for positive body image and the fat-acceptance movement, Cateyes posted a photo of herself in a blue bikini online to make a statement about accepting her body as it was. She was horrified when she discovered that her photo was being used in a diet company's Facebook ads as the "before" picture. "It made me feel exposed and not in control of my own image," says Cateyes. "I'm used to negative attention [online], but for somebody to make money off of me? That really infuriated me."[10] When Cateyes contacted the diet company, she was told that a third-party affiliate was responsible for using her image. The company is working to find and remove ads with her image online. Cateyes has vowed to keep working to find and report remaining images of herself in the diet ads. "I'm definitely not going to stop making a stink about it,"[11] she says.

In response to rising privacy concerns, many social media users have realized that leaving social media accounts open to the public, like Cateyes did on her blog, opens the door to having their information used in ways they do not want. Therefore, many actively manage their accounts to control privacy and the flow of information. According to a 2013 survey of more than two thousand US adults, commissioned by security firm ESET and conducted by Harris Interactive, four out of five people changed the privacy settings on their social media accounts, with most having made changes within the previous six months.

Users' Contradictory Behavior

Although many people say they value privacy and are actively managing their social media accounts, the decisions they make while using social media sometimes contradict and hinder the goal of privacy. Users voluntarily provide personal information on social media sites. They use location services to post and share where they are at any moment. They upload pictures of new purchases or vacation locales. And sometimes, they ignore warnings that their private information has been accessed.

In 2010 web security expert Gary LosHuertos sat in a New York City café and tested how people reacted to privacy breaches on social media. He used a software tool that allowed him to snoop on people as they used free wireless Internet in the café. Within a few minutes, LosHuertos was able to access the accounts of more than a dozen people on Facebook. He used the people's own Facebook accounts to send them a warning message, telling them that he had hacked their accounts and knew where they were. Although LosHuertos expected a furious reaction to his privacy invasions, many of his targets continued surfing the Internet and Facebook as if nothing had happened. LosHuertos sent a second message. Still, nothing happened. With access to their Facebook accounts, he knew that the targets had read his messages, but they continued online as if no one were watching them. "What's absolutely incomprehensible is that after someone has been alerted to the danger that they would casually ignore the warning, and continue about their day,"[12] says LosHuertos.

Privacy expert Alessandro Acquisti believes some users' contradictory behavior may be rooted in a sense of helplessness over social media privacy. He explains:

> There are so many mental steps we have to go through. Do I even know there is a potential privacy risk? If I do, do I know [if] there are alternative strategies, such as adjusting privacy settings? Do I know, or at least feel, that these will be effective, or are they a waste of time? And then, if they are effective, are they too costly in terms of time or effect? After all that, I may very well decide not to take those steps.[13]

Many social media users take advantage of free wireless Internet connections in coffee shops and other venues. These connections can be risky; they leave users open to privacy breaches.

The Harris survey supports the finding that although users say they value privacy, their behavior contradicts this statement. The poll found that almost two-thirds of respondents said individuals should be primarily responsible for privacy on social media. "However, when we probed further into online behavior, particularly around social media, it became clear that putting that belief into practice remains challenging," says Stephen Cobb, researcher and survey author. "For example, more than half of U.S. adult social media users say they have not read the most recent privacy policy for their social accounts."[14] And while the Harris poll found that approximately four in five people changed their social media privacy settings, there were still 20 percent who had never changed the privacy settings for their social media accounts at all. "Lack of attention to privacy and security on social media does seem to be at odds with the belief in individual responsibility. This is even more surprising when you consider the negative experiences of more than a few users," says Cobb. "It is hard to think that everyone who leaves the default settings in place is aware of the implications."[15]

Privacy Versus Control

According to security technologist Bruce Schneier, users' contradictory behavior on social media may not mean that they do not value privacy. Instead, he says users are more concerned with controlling the flow of personal information. "Privacy is about control," he explains. "When a social networking site changes your privacy settings to make what used to be visible only to your friends visible to everyone . . . your loss of control over that information is the issue. We may not mind sharing our personal lives and thoughts, but we want to control how, where and with whom. A privacy failure is a control failure."[16]

In 2011 Facebook executives announced that they had added more privacy controls to help protect users' personal information. "It is all about making it easier to share with exactly who you want and never be surprised about who sees something,"[17] Chris Cox, Facebook's vice president of product, said in 2011 as the site unveiled the new controls. Yet privacy experts maintain that loopholes still exist on the site that threaten users' control over private information. For example, friends can post information and pictures about other users without consent, and users cannot remove it.

Social Media Anywhere, Anytime

With the rising popularity of smartphones and tablets, users are logging on to social media anywhere they go. A 2012 report from comScore, an Internet technology company, found that social media users spent more time accessing social media via mobile devices than they did through desktop computers or laptops. In March 2012 Facebook users spent more than seven hours on mobile browsers or apps, compared to six hours on the computer. Twitter users spent more than two hours on the site on mobile devices and only twenty minutes via a traditional computer. Robert DeFelice, vice president on the media team for GfK, a research company, points out:

> Reading in-the-moment status updates and posting short comments, replies and *like*s are activities tailor-made for smartphones. Apps encourage a targeted, deliberate approach to online time that consumers may not even clearly associate with "the Internet." On a PC, by contrast, people open browsers to access social media, email, and a variety of other sites; but their interest in going beyond a familiar repertoire of activities, even on the PC, seems to be dwindling.

Quoted in "Social Media Dominates Smartphone Internet Time, Accounting for Almost One-Third of Minutes," Business Wire, December 17, 2012. www.businesswire.com.

Facebook's controls did not protect Bobbi Duncan, a student at the University of Texas, who did not want her father to find out that she was a lesbian. She was open about her sexuality on campus, but hid it from her conservative family. Duncan adjusted her Facebook privacy settings to hide any information about her sexuality from her father, who she knew was on Facebook. "Once I had my Facebook settings set, I knew—or thought I knew— there wasn't any problem,"[18] she says. When she joined a school choir group called the Queer Chorus in 2012, the choir's president added Duncan to the choir's Facebook discussion group. This unknowingly exposed Duncan's sexuality by posting a note to her nearly two hundred Facebook friends, including her father, that she had joined the Queer Chorus. Within a few hours, Duncan's father had left her angry voice mails and demanded that she renounce same-sex relationships. Duncan remembers telling a friend, "I have him hidden from my updates, but he saw this. He saw it." Duncan says that the social media site should take more responsibility for ensuring that users have control over their information. "I blame Facebook," she says. "It shouldn't be somebody else's choice what people see of me."[19]

> "I blame Facebook. It shouldn't be somebody else's choice what people see of me."[19]
>
> —Bobbi Duncan, a University of Texas student whose personal information was exposed on Facebook.

Are Privacy Concerns Overblown?

Not everyone agrees social media is eroding privacy values, instead claiming the key to social media and privacy coexisting is control. danah boyd is an Internet researcher who specializes in social media. She believes that when users fully understand their audience and the potential usage of their information on social media, they can make informed privacy decisions and control their information. With control, privacy on social media becomes less of a concern.

She explains:

> People of all ages care deeply about privacy. And they care just as much about privacy online as they do offline. But what privacy means may not be what you think. Fundamentally, privacy is about having control over how information flows. It's about being able to understand the social setting in order to behave appropriately. To do so, people must trust their interpretation of the context, including the people in the room and the architecture that defines the setting. When they feel as though control has been taken away from them or when they lack the control they need to do the right thing, they scream privacy foul.[20]

Chapter 2

Sharing Information Online

In the summer of 2013, National Public Radio host Scott Simon grieved by his dying mother's hospital bedside and said goodbye to her. In the final days of his mother's life, Scott also revealed his feelings to his 1.2 million Twitter followers. "I love holding my mother's hand. Haven't held it like this since I was 9. Why did I stop? I thought it unmanly? What crap,"[21] he said in one tweet. In the age of social media, stories like Simon's are not unusual. Social media sites have made it easy for people to post deeply personal information online, even at some of the most difficult times of their lives.

Sharing Personal Details

People have been disclosing personal information since long before the Internet and social media. In a 2011 study conducted by the *New York Times* about the psychology of online sharing, a female participant explains, "In the past, people shared [their thoughts] at lunch with their girlfriends when they saw someone with something cool." The introduction of the Internet and social media has simply created a new avenue for people to divulge information. "We still share things when it's relevant . . . we just share more and online,"[22] she says.

Popular sites such as Facebook, LinkedIn, Instagram, Twitter, and Vine work by allowing people to create a web of friends and acquaintances, sometimes called followers. Online, users can post their thoughts, photos, videos, whereabouts, contact information, and interests for their network of friends to see.

Revealing personal information online has become a global phenomenon, with people around the world posting details about their lives for others to see. According to a 2013 poll by market and opinion research firm Ipsos, 71 percent of people online in 24 countries had posted content on social media sites within the month before the poll. Many, like danah boyd, use multiple social media sites, sometimes having multiple accounts on the same platform. boyd says that she has several Twitter accounts. "I have both my formal, professional @ zephoria account, but then I also have a personal account which is me joking around with friends—and then I have an even sillier account which is me pretending to be my 7-month-old son," says boyd. "Flickr has been a home for a long time to share photos with friends."[23] boyd says that she also spends time on LinkedIn and Facebook.

When sharing online, users post a variety of content. Pictures are the most popular item, with 43 percent of respondents in the Ipsos poll reporting they had posted pictures online in the past month. People also post other information, including their opinions, status updates about what they are doing or how they are feeling, links to articles they find interesting, products or services they recommend, news items of interest, video clips, and plans for future activities and trips. The content people post frequently includes personal details that could be used to identify them. According to a 2013 report from Trend Micro, 63 percent of social media users post their birthday, while 51 percent reveal the names of family members and pets. Users also share location information, such as hometowns, schools, and vacation plans. Some types of social media users are more likely to post information. Factors that make people more likely to share online include gender, education level, and income level. According to the 2013 Ipsos poll, women are slightly more likely than men to share content, and people with a high level of education are also slightly more likely to post personal information online than those with a low to medium education level. The Ipsos poll revealed that income level is another predictor of social media use; users with a high income are slightly more likely to share personal details than those with medium or low income.

Teens Online

Teens and young adults have grown up with computers and the Internet. As a result, they are typically more comfortable putting the details

Teens are among the most frequent users of social media sites. Because they are so comfortable with social media, they sometimes share too much personal information with friends and other users.

of their lives online than older individuals. According to a 2013 report from the Pew Research Internet Project, eight out of ten online teens use social media. Ninety-four percent of teen social media users are on Facebook, while 26 percent have a Twitter account. Instagram is also a growing favorite, attracting 11 percent of teens on social media.

Teens are typically very active on social media. Almost half of teen social media users say that they visit sites several times per day. An additional 25 percent of teens say they use social media daily. Girls and older teens are the most active users of social media sites, with almost half checking sites multiple times per day.

Like adults, many teens are active on multiple social media sites, using each for different purposes and audiences. "I am basically dividing things up," says one sixteen-year-old female participant in the Pew study. "Instagram is mostly for pictures. Twitter is mostly for just saying what you are thinking. Facebook is both of them combined so you have to give a little bit of each. But . . . I posted more pictures on Instagram than on Facebook. Twitter is more natural."[24]

Teens have become so comfortable on social media that they are sharing more personal information than they did even a few years ago. In a 2013 Pew study, researchers found that teen social media users were significantly more likely to share personal information in 2012 than they were in 2006. The researchers also noted that as teens aged, their use of social media changed. Younger teens were more likely to have smaller networks and not to post as much personal content. As they grew older, teens were more likely to become frequent social media users, have larger networks of friends, and post a wide variety of content.

Motivated to Share

The motivation that drives people to share intimate details of their lives online differs from person to person. To understand the primary motivations behind sharing online, researchers with the *New York Times* Customer Insight Group conducted a study called "The Psychology of Sharing." In the study, researchers identified five primary motivations for sharing. Some people share to bring valuable and entertaining content to others. They might post links to articles they enjoyed or video clips they found humorous. "I share to enrich the lives of those around me,"[25] says one study participant. Ninety-four percent of those surveyed reported that they carefully consider how the information they share would be useful to those reading or viewing it.

> "I share to enrich the lives of those around me."[25]
>
> —*A participant in a* New York Times *study about the motivations of sharing online.*

Others are motivated to share on social media because it helps them define themselves to others. They might post information about a job promotion, an opinion piece, or support for a particular political candidate. Sixty-eight percent of participants said that they share to give people a better sense of who they are and what they care about. Some participants said that they share only information that reinforces the image that they want to project online.

Finding Fame on Social Media

As many as one-third of teens and tweens who use social media may be more concerned with fame than with privacy. A survey conducted of youth aged nine to fifteen by the University of California–Los Angeles's Children's Digital Media Center found that 33 percent of young people surveyed said being famous was somewhat important, important, or very important. Researchers also found that young people who use social media place a higher value on fame than those who do not use it. "Kids who claim they want to be famous use more media," says lead author Yalda Uhls, one of the researchers on the study.

Teens looking for fame can point to several examples of people who themselves used social media to achieve it. Singer Justin Bieber launched his career by posting on YouTube a video of himself singing, which led to him being discovered in 2008 at age thirteen. In 2010 twelve-year-old Greyson Chance from Edmond, Oklahoma, posted a video of himself singing and playing piano on YouTube. Within months, the video had gathered thousands of fans. Television talk show host Ellen DeGeneres saw it and invited him to Los Angeles to perform on her show. Chance later signed a record deal and released a debut album in 2011.

Psychologists say that social media encourages fame-seeking behavior from tweens and teens. "Fame-seeking is not new," says psychologist Carl Pickhardt. "What's new is you can actualize part of that. You can post pictures and data about yourself. All of a sudden, you can imitate what it's like to be famous."

Quoted in Sharon Jayson, "Survey: Young People Who Use Social Media Seek Fame," *USA Today*, April 18, 2013. www.usatoday.com.

Sharing to keep in touch with others and grow personal relationships is another motivator for social media users. Vacation photos, status updates, and funny anecdotes about daily life can make people feel close, even if they are geographically separated. A significant number, 78 percent, said that they share personal information online because it helps them stay connected with people that they might not otherwise keep in touch with.

Sharing also provides a feeling of self-fulfillment for many social media users. "I enjoy getting comments that I sent great information and that my friends will forward it to their friends because it's so helpful. It makes me feel valuable,"[26] says a female study participant. Others use social media as an avenue to spread news about causes, brands, products, or services that they support or recommend. In fact, 84 percent of study participants reported that they use social media to support the causes and issues they feel strongly about.

Privacy Boundaries Slipping

While the nature of social media encourages people to share personal information, there is a growing concern that sharing online is eroding personal privacy. Privacy advocates warn that the Internet provides a sense of anonymity that may influence a user's decision on how much information to reveal. When online, people may not use the same amount of restraint that they might use when they meet and talk to an acquaintance in person. In addition, users may also share information specifically intended for friends, forgetting that a wider audience may be reading or viewing their posts. When this occurs, information that was meant to be private may be unknowingly spread to a public audience.

> "When you become active in social networks, you probably have reached the conclusion that this privacy thing isn't all that important. You probably think it's a little bit of hype."[27]
>
> —*Larry Ponemon, chair and founder of the Ponemon Institute.*

Recent research supports the idea that users are becoming more open on social media. A survey by the Ponemon Institute conducted for MSNBC in 2011 found that avid social media users were less concerned about privacy than in 2006. Researchers concluded that frequent use of social media sites like Facebook and Twitter calmed people's concerns about privacy. "When you become active in social networks, you probably have reached the conclusion that this privacy thing isn't all that important," says Larry Ponemon, who conducted the survey. "You probably think it's a little bit of hype."[27]

Privacy Management

Supporters of social media claim that privacy fears are unfounded because most social media sites give users a certain amount of control over their online privacy. Most sites allow users to manage control settings and make privacy decisions about who sees the information they post. More than half of social media users take advantage of these controls and take some measures to manage their privacy on social media. According to a 2012 Pew Internet Research Project report titled "Privacy Management on Social Media Sites," 58 percent of social networking site users restrict access to their profiles, making their profile private and allowing only friends to view their posts. Only 20 percent of users say they set their main profile to be completely public. Women are more likely than men are to set their profiles to private: 67 percent versus 48 percent.

For those who already restrict access to their profile, some also take additional steps to manage their social media accounts. Twenty-six percent of those who have already restricted their profile in some way report that they use additional controls to limit what certain groups of friends see.

Social media users also take specific steps to protect their privacy and control their information. Many users actively manage their profiles by deleting friends, deleting comments from others on their profiles, and untagging themselves from another user's posts or pictures.

Confusion over Privacy

Despite efforts to manage privacy, there are times when private information shared on social media goes beyond its intended audience. Sometimes privacy leaks occur when users mismanage or forget to turn on privacy settings. Other times users want to restrict privacy but find they are confused about how to do it. Research by Pew Internet has found almost half of social media users (48 percent) admit to having difficulty with social media privacy controls.

For a small number of users, concerns over privacy have led them to stop using social media altogether. A survey of three hundred Facebook users and three hundred who have quit the site by psychologists at the University of Vienna in Austria found that among those who

The Value of Personal Data

Personal data has become very valuable online. Social media sites are only one of a number of companies that track the online activities of customers to gain a competitive edge. These companies use this information themselves or sell it to third parties. Data brokers are companies that collect thousands of details on almost every American adult. Data brokers know what users buy, their race, finances, health, social networks, and web-browsing habits. This personal information can be used to rank consumers. Some consumers are ranked as high value and receive marketing and offers for premium credit cards and other valuable items. Other users are labeled as a waste of time. Companies spend little marketing money and effort targeting them. Personal data can also be used to profile users and group them into specific categories. Access to these groups of consumers can be sold to marketers buying ad space online.

Companies that track consumers online argue that their practices lead to a better, more personalized Internet experience for users. Others believe that these companies and social media sites have crossed the line, violating Internet users' right to privacy.

quit Facebook, almost half left because of privacy concerns. "Many of them seemed to be concerned about privacy to such an extent that it outweighed perceived advantages of Facebook and eventually led them to quit their virtual Facebook identity,"[28] says Stefan Stieger, the study's lead researcher.

Tracking User Activity

Even when users are using social media privacy controls adequately, their personal information may be seen by more people than they realize. Behind the scenes, social media sites are tracking what millions of users do online. When users log in to their Facebook accounts, the company records the user's name, e-mail address, friends, and all of

Social media sites such as Facebook track the online activities of their users for a variety of reasons, including for advertising purposes. These sites also try to make users aware of external threats to privacy, as can be seen on this Facebook Security page.

the data in the user's profile. The site keeps logs that record the past ninety days of activity for each user. In addition, Facebook inserts tracking cookies in users' browsers. Each time the user visits a third-party website that has a Facebook "Like" button or Facebook plug-in, the button or plug in-works with the cookie and tells Facebook the date, time, and web address of the page the user has visited. It also records identifying characteristics of the user's computer and browser, such as IP address, operating system, and browser version. With so much information about a user's web searches and online browsing habits, social media sites can create a detailed profile of a user that includes political affiliations, religious beliefs, sexual orientation, or health issues.

Social media sites make money by selling ad space to companies that want to reach their users. They use the information they have collected on users to tailor ads to specific audiences. For example, advertisers may select key details like relationship status, location, activities, or favorite books. Then sites like Facebook run the ads for a targeted group of users who fit the desired profile. Social media sites say that tracking users is valuable because it helps them tailor online ads to each user based on their interests, creating a personalized experience on the web. For example, a person who looks at websites that sell exercise equipment will very likely see ads automatically pop up for exercise equipment the next time he or she goes online.

This type of online behavioral or targeted advertising is growing fast on social media and other websites. Advertisers are willing to spend more money to place ads in front of targeted groups of users who are more likely to be interested in the products and services being advertised. "More data means better targeting, which means more revenue,"[29] says Marissa Gluck, managing partner of the media consulting firm Radar Research. As a result, social media sites face increasing financial pressure to collect and store more user data. Privacy advocates warn that too much personal information collected in the hands of social media sites or sold to third parties violates user privacy.

> "Many of them seemed to be concerned about privacy to such an extent that it outweighed perceived advantages of Facebook and eventually led them to quit their virtual Facebook identity."[28]
>
> —*Stefan Stieger, a psychologist and researcher at the University of Vienna.*

Researchers and Privacy

In addition to user tracking by the sites themselves, an army of researchers also collects data on social media every time a user tweets to Twitter followers or shares something new on Facebook. Every step on social media creates a digital footprint that researchers use in their latest studies. For example, Facebook has studied how parents and kids interact from posts on its network.

As huge amounts of digital data are collected for research, some people are concerned that the practice is a violation of user privacy and that users may not approve of their behavior being studied. Social psychologist Ilka Gleibs, assistant professor at the London School of Economics and Political Science, studies social networking sites and cautions users to be aware that these sites are being watched. "Sometimes it's easier than we think to identify this data," she says. "I'm not saying no one should ever do this kind of research, but I'm saying we should be more cautious when we use this data."[30]

Others, like privacy expert Parry Aftab, say that users do not need to worry about researchers using their social media data, because the large social media sites have privacy policies that protect users. "The sites will never provide personally identifiable information unless they have the consent of the users. And there is legal recourse if they're using it in any other way,"[31] says Aftab.

Balancing Social Media and Privacy

Social media has become a new platform for people from all cultures and countries to share thoughts, feelings, and information. At the same time, there is a growing concern over what happens to information once it is placed online. Participating in social media while still protecting online privacy has become a delicate balancing act, one that users must manage with every click online.

Chapter 3

Public Versus Private Lives

In November 2011 Patrick Snay, the former headmaster at Gulliver Preparatory School in Miami, won an age discrimination lawsuit against the school. The court awarded Snay a settlement of $80,000. The settlement also contained a standard confidentiality clause, which prohibited Snay or the school from talking about the case.

After Snay told his daughter Dana about the settlement, she bragged to her twelve hundred Facebook friends, "Mama and Papa Snay won the case against Gulliver. Gulliver is now officially paying for my vacation to Europe this summer."[32] Many of those friends were current and former Gulliver students, and news of the post quickly made its way to the school's lawyers. They notified Snay that the school would not pay the $80,000 settlement because he had violated the confidentiality agreement. An appeals court agreed with Gulliver and tossed out the discrimination settlement in January 2014.

Although Snay can appeal the decision to the Florida Supreme Court, attorney Bradley Shear says his chances of winning the settlement back are small. "It depends on the terms of the confidentiality contract; each one is different, but the damage is likely done," says Shear. "Some confidentiality agreements stipulate that the client cannot tell people who are not involved in the case: others prohibit anyone from knowing. Facebook is a public forum, even if her profile is set to private, and that's where the mistake was made." Shear says that if Snay's daughter had not posted on social media, the settlement would probably not have been thrown out. "The bottom line is, when involved in legal proceedings, don't disclose anything on social media. It's not worth it,"[33] he says.

As the Snays learned firsthand, the line between private and public lives can become blurred on social media. While most social media users are comfortable with authorized sharing and use of their information, privacy concerns emerge when personal details spread beyond the intended audience or are used in unintended or unauthorized ways. Sometimes, when private information goes public on social media, serious consequences result.

Damaging Reputations

Most people change their behavior for different situations. A nursery school teacher behaves and dresses differently for her young class than she does when going out to celebrate a friend's birthday. Teens say and do things with their friends that they would hold back in front of their grandparents. In the real world most people are able to manage these different personas, choosing the appropriate behaviors, words, and dress for each situation.

Because social media makes people feel close and connected to friends, it is easy to forget that anything posted online may be seen by the public. An off-color joke that is funny to a small group of friends might not be appreciated by a future employer. Pictures of a wild night of partying might be seen negatively by school officials, employers, parents, and others. While social media posts take only a few seconds to create, when seen by the wrong audience, they can have a long-lasting impact on a user's reputation.

At St. Mary's University in Halifax, Nova Scotia, several football players were suspended in early 2014 because of offensive tweets that contained sexist, racist, and homophobic language. One of the students involved in the controversy, Rhys Tansley, said in a message to the Canadian Press that one of his tweets was written while he was working as a security guard at a bar. A disruptive woman he was escorting out of the business bit his arm and spit in his face. "I was angry about what happened. I do what the majority of young adults do and expressed my emotions and thoughts on twitter,"[34] he wrote. Despite his explanations, the damage has already been done to Tansley's and the others' reputations. J.P. Rains, an official at Laurentian University in Ontario, Canada, says students need to realize social media posts can have long-lasting consequences and every time they use Twitter,

Facebook, and other social media they should be aware of the potential impact on their future.

Adults of all ages, occupations, and social classes have also run into trouble when private social media posts become public. In 2011 New York representative Anthony Weiner was forced to resign when the public learned he had sent lewd messages and pictures of his anatomy to women on Twitter. Weiner attempted to send the messages privately to a single user. Instead, they went to tens of thousands of his Twitter followers and were retweeted to even more. In 2013 Weiner ran into trouble on social media again when his sexual photos and messages under the pseudonym "Carlos Danger" appeared on another social media platform called Formspring, causing the politician to exit the race for New York City mayor. Social media allowed Weiner's

Social media users who send or post sexually suggestive photos and messages open themselves to public ridicule—or worse. Former New York representative Anthony Weiner (pictured) has experienced this firsthand.

messages to become public and spread quickly. "People still think and behave as though they are communicating one-to-one, when in fact, digital communication is a volatile and shareable thing,"[35] says Susan Etlinger, an analyst with the Altimeter Group.

Sometimes employees can find out the hard way how harmful an ill-advised post on social media can be. In 2013 Justine Sacco was the head of corporate communications for IAC, a media company. When she was about to board a flight to South Africa, she tweeted a quick message, "Going to Africa. Hope I don't get AIDS. Just kidding. I'm white!"[36] Sacco's Twitter account had only about five hundred followers, but the offensive message soon went viral and triggered a social media frenzy. Before Sacco's twelve-hour flight had even landed, her employer had learned of the tweet. The next day, Sacco was terminated from her job with IAC. The company issued a statement: "The offensive comment does not reflect the views and values of IAC. We take this issue very seriously, and we have parted ways with the employee in question. There is no excuse for the hateful statements that have been made and we condemn them unequivocally."[37]

> "People still think and behave as though they are communicating one-to-one, when in fact, digital communication is a volatile and shareable thing."[35]
>
> —Susan Etlinger, an analyst with the Altimeter Group.

Colleges Watching Prospective Students

Like adults, teens are discovering the consequences that can happen when private online posts become public. For generations, teens have done or said something they later regretted. Before computers and the Internet, only the small number of people who were present knew what happened or what was said. Today, however, virtually every detail of a teen's life can appear on the Internet, put on social media by them or by their friends. Even if teens are careful about posting only appropriate content, a friend may tag them in a picture from an underage drinking party or other compromising situation. Suddenly, people who do not even know the teen can see what he or she has done. Within a few minutes, a momentary lapse in judgment can become permanent online.

Protect Your Social Media Reputation

Today a single tweet or Facebook photo can ruin a user's chances of getting a job or being admitted to college. To help users protect their social media reputation, a new tool called Persona monitors users' social media presence. The tool flags and notifies users about questionable posts and content before they cause a problem. Persona's filters look for items that can give a negative impact when a user applies for a job or college. Negative items could include references to illegal drugs, sexual posts, profanity, poor grammar and spelling, and alcohol consumption. If Persona finds a negative item, it notifies the user, who is then able to delete the potentially damaging material.

Kieran Wiseman is a senior at Central Washington University. He says that he uses the text-only version of Persona. He had originally decided to delete his Facebook account entirely because of privacy concerns while he was job hunting. But Wiseman reconsidered when professors told him that deleting his entire account might be a red flag for potential employers. Instead, he decided to use Persona to clean up his social media accounts. "Viewing my post on Persona rather than Facebook or Twitter takes them out of context, which shows how they could be misconstrued as inappropriate," says Wiseman "I have deleted some things I originally thought weren't bad until I saw them on Persona."

Quoted in Annie Johnson, "New Tool Aims to Protect Your Social Media Reputation," *USA Today*, November 7, 2013. www.usatoday.com.

For high school seniors applying to college, a seemingly harmless post can affect their college admission prospects. According to Kaplan Test Prep's 2012 College Admissions Officers Survey, colleges are increasingly using social media to recruit students. Eighty-seven percent of the colleges surveyed said they used Facebook and 76 percent used Twitter to recruit students. While on social media sites, admissions officers can find information that could jeopardize a student's application. In fact, 35 percent of admissions officers who did an Internet search on an applicant or visited the applicant's Facebook page said they found something that negatively affected the student's application to the school. "Students' social media and digital footprint can sometimes play a role in the admissions process," says Christine Brown, the executive director of K–12 and college prep programs at Kaplan Test Prep. "It's something that is becoming more ubiquitous and less looked down upon."[38]

At Pitzer College in Claremont, California, for example, a prospective student sabotaged his chance at admission with a social media post. An undergraduate at Pitzer friended the student on Facebook and noticed that the student had posted offensive comments about a high school teacher. The undergraduate notified Pitzer's admissions office, which considered the social media post when reviewing the student's application. "We thought, this is not the kind of person we want in our community," says Angel B. Perez, Pitzer's dean of admission and financial aid. "We didn't admit the student."[39]

> "Students' social media and digital footprint can sometimes play a role in the admissions process."[38]
>
> —Christine Brown, executive director of K–12 and college prep programs at Kaplan Test Prep.

Some colleges like Colgate University in New York notify students if they are rejected for reasons other than academics. "We should be transparent with applicants," says Gary L. Ross, Colgate's dean of admissions. In one example, Colgate accepted a student but then learned via social media of an alcohol-related incident. Ross called the student to verify if the incident was true. When the student confirmed that it was, Colgate rescinded its offer of admission to the student. "We will always ask if there is something we didn't understand,"[40] says Ross.

To help teens avoid social media pitfalls when applying to college, high school guidance counselors are advising them how to clean up their online profiles. "They imagine admissions officers are old professors. But we tell them a lot of admissions officers are very young and technology-savvy,"[41] says Lenny Libenzon, the guidance department chair at Brookline High School in Massachusetts. Some of the strategies that teens are learning to clean up their online image include deleting alcohol-related content, removing potentially offen-

A young man answers questions during a job interview. Job recruiters and some employers routinely check the online presence of prospective employees.

sive language, and creating socially acceptable e-mail addresses. They are also learning to change their names on Facebook to something that is not easily searchable and untag themselves in friends' pictures.

Risking Careers

Like college admissions officers, employers are also researching job applicants and monitoring current employees on social media. Jobvite's 2013 social recruiting survey revealed that recruiters are increasingly using a job candidate's social profile as part of the hiring process. In the survey, 93 percent of recruiters said they reviewed a potential employee's online presence. What they found online caused 42 percent of recruiters to reconsider a candidate. Recruiters said they reacted negatively to mentions of doing illegal drugs, sexual posts, profanity, and spelling or grammatical errors. On the other hand, when recruiters found favorable posts or tweets about volunteering and charitable donations, they viewed the job candidate in a more positive light.

Tracking on Twitter

Varsity Monitor offers a simple service to major universities: It will keep an online eye on the school's athletes. The company uses a computer application that searches social media sites for obscenities, offensive comments, or words like *free* that may indicate the athlete has violated National Collegiate Athletic Association (NCAA) rules by accepting a gift. Major universities such as North Carolina, Nebraska, and Oklahoma pay $7,000 to $10,000 annually for Varsity Monitor's watchful eye. "Every school, we work to customize their keyword list," says Sam Carnahan, the chief executive of Varsity Monitor. "We look for things that could damage the school's brand and anything related to their eligibility."

Schools are turning to companies like Varsity Monitor to help them avoid trouble when an athlete posts something on social media that could cause problems for the athlete or the school. In March 2012 North Carolina's football program received a one-year ban from bowl games and lost fifteen scholarships after a Twitter message sent by a player triggered an NCAA investigation. Some believe that schools have a responsibility to track public information put on social media by students if there is a suspicion that team or league rules have been violated. To do so, some schools require athletes to hand over access to social media accounts. Others caution that monitoring student accounts can violate online privacy. "There's this big gray area that we're all going into right now," says Bill Voth, cofounder of Spiracle Media, a company that advises colleges about social media. "Schools like North Carolina need to protect themselves. But I can see the legal side with privacy issues."

Quoted in Pete Thamel, "Tracking Twitter, Raising Red Flags," *New York Times*, March 30, 2012. www.nytimes.com.

Young people in particular are risking future careers because of social media profiles. Many young people create a social media presence to be seen by friends, not thinking about potential employers viewing the same information. For some, this mistake may cost them a job. According to a 2013 report by On Device Research, one in ten people aged sixteen to thirty-four have not been offered a new job because of photos or comments on Facebook, Twitter, and other social media sites. "If getting a job wasn't hard enough in this tough economic climate, young people are getting rejected from employment because of their social media profiles and they are not concerned about it,"[42] says On Device Research's marketing manager Sarah Quinn.

Sometimes, an innocent personal photo can damage a career. In 2009 twenty-four-year-old high school teacher Ashley Payne posted a picture on Facebook from her European vacation showing her holding a pint of beer and a glass of red wine. She believed it to be a harmless photo until her principal called her into his office and told her that a parent had complained. He gave Payne a choice: resign or be suspended. Payne resigned. She says that she feels that she did nothing wrong. She used the privacy setting on her Facebook account and thought that only her closest friends would see the vacation photos. Payne says:

"If getting a job wasn't hard enough in this tough economic climate, young people are getting rejected from employment because of their social media profiles and they are not concerned about it."[42]

—*Sarah Quinn, On Device Research marketing manager.*

> Facebook is not the classroom. And it's not open to the students of my classroom. They are not supposed to see it. I have privacy in place so they don't see it. . . . Yes, I put it on the Internet, so you can make that argument. But it sort of feels like the same thing as if I had put the pictures in a shoebox in my house and someone came in and took them and showed one of them to the principal.[43]

Payne's experience serves as a warning to social media users that even what they think is private may be public. Even when a user is careful, social media posts may not be private, says author Frederick S. Lane. "All it takes is one person making a copy of what you've posted and it's out in the wild, and you no longer have that control,"[44] he says.

When an employee gripes about a boss or picky customers to friends after work, such comments are private and usually harmless. If the employee puts those same comments on social media, however, not everyone may appreciate their humor. In 2013 Matt Watson was fired from his job at a Seattle coffee shop after it was revealed that he was the Bitter Barista blogger. As the Bitter Barista, Watson blogged sarcastic comments about his customers and his boss such as, "I would remember your usual drink if you were a more memorable person," and "I like to use a lot of big words when I tweet, that way if my boss ever finds my twitter account, he won't understand any of it."[45] Watson says that the blog was meant to be satire and he was simply highlighting the small percentage of customers who make a barista's job more difficult. He did not post his name or the name of the shop where he worked. But there were enough hints that within a few weeks, Watson was outed online as the blogger and fired. His boss, Seth Levy, did not appreciate the comments, even if they were meant as satire. "He was writing about his boss during business hours," says Levy. "I represent the business, the customers and the staff. I can't endorse what he was saying, whether humorous or not. It puts me in a difficult position, where if I don't respond that means I endorse what he's saying."[46]

Blurred Boundaries

Sometimes, the line between public and private information online becomes blurred. When users decide to open up online, they can expose themselves to criticism from others. In 2013 sixteen-year-old Hannah Anderson demonstrated the blurring boundaries between social media and privacy when she shared intimate details about her abduction. Anderson had been taken hostage by family friend James DiMaggio, who was accused by police of killing her mother and younger brother. A week later the teen was rescued at a lakeside campsite in the Idaho wilderness; DiMaggio was killed in a shootout with police. Days after her rescue, Anderson turned to the social media website Ask.fm and answered questions from the public about her ordeal. Ask.fm is a question-and-answer social media site where people ask users anything they want. In Anderson's case she responded

38

In answer to questions on a social media site, Hannah Anderson (pictured) shared intimate details about her 2013 abduction. Some say this represents a blurring of boundaries.

to questions such as "Why didn't you run?" and "How did he separate you from your mom and brother?" Anderson also posted a picture of herself online.

Some mental health experts questioned the teen's decision to share the intimately personal details on social media. "This is a 16-year-old who's totally traumatized, she's in a state of trauma and so she's not thinking," says psychotherapist Wendy Walsh. "Sometimes in a numb state, you do things that you don't really consider the consequences."[47]

By making such intimate details public, Anderson raised suspicions among many in the public that her version of the abduction might not be entirely accurate. Author Chelsea Hoffman has analyzed many high-profile kidnapping cases, including the Anderson case. She says that Anderson's behavior raises suspicions that her story may be quite different from what actually happened. "I can't really think of any notable survivors of kidnappings that shared the same behavior as she has," says Hoffman, who released a book on the Anderson kidnapping in 2013. "Elizabeth Smart, Jaycee Dugard, Amanda Berry . . . the only time any of these people have really spoken to the public in the beginning was to ask for privacy and peace while they picked up the pieces of their lives and healed."[48]

No Guarantees

Although social media can be a positive place to connect with friends and discover new information, users need to be careful about the personal information they choose to share. Online privacy is never guaranteed. Comments and posts meant for a select few can live forever publicly on the Internet. Being aware of the risks of sharing personal information online can help users better control their information on social media.

Chapter 4

Scams and
Threats

In 2014 Michael DiCarlo's ninety-two-year old grandmother received an international call. The caller pretended to be DiCarlo and told her that he had been kidnapped in Mexico. "Someone posing as me got on the phone and I was very, the person was very upset. . . . My grandmother said the voice was muffled so she couldn't really tell if it was me or not. The person was crying and said, 'Nonna, please just send the money,'"[49] says DiCarlo. His grandmother believed the caller because he used Michael's special nickname for his grandmother. She went to the bank and tried to wire $1,900, but the wire transfer failed. As she later discovered, the entire kidnapping story was fake.

In recent years this type of scam has tricked thousands of people. International thieves scroll through social media accounts to gather personal information that can be used against users and their family members. Investigators believe that in DiCarlo's case, the con man probably gathered his personal information, including his grandmother's nickname, from his Facebook account.

For many victims, this scam is costly. One businessman wired $2,000 to London after receiving an e-mail purportedly from his niece, saying she had lost her wallet and passport. The e-mail was fraudulent, but the criminals knew the niece was in London because she had checked in on Facebook. Using such personal details, these criminals create a sense of urgency for their victims and ask them to send money for a made-up crisis. "And that sense you don't know what's happening around you and that's what they bank on, they want you to leave your house immediately and get to a Western Union place and wire the money,"[50] says Steve Bernas, a representative from the Better Business Bureau.

As DiCarlo's experience illustrates, sharing information on social media can be dangerous. A user may put information online for friends and family, but online scammers and stalkers also lurk on social media and use these sites to target victims.

Online Scams

Scammers from snake oil salesmen to pool hall hustlers have tricked victims out of money for centuries. With the power of the Internet, however, these crooks can reach billions of potential victims with a few clicks of a mouse. Social media sites are particularly fruitful for con men because they encourage sharing, which spreads a scammer's message farther than ever before.

With 1.23 billion users as of the end of 2013, Facebook is a gold mine for many online scammers, who can easily find valuable information by scrolling through user profiles. "If you tell me your date of birth and where you're born [on Facebook] I'm 98 percent to stealing your identity," says con-man-turned-FBI-security-expert Frank Abagnale. "Never state your date of birth and where you were born, otherwise you are saying 'come and steal my identity.'" He also recommends never using a passport-style photo for a Facebook profile picture, instead opting for a safer group photo. "What [people] say on a Facebook page stays with them. Every time you say you 'like' or 'don't like' you are telling someone your sexual orientation, ethnic background, voting record,"[51] he says.

On social media, online scammers take advantage of the relationships people have with others. Some scams use fake messages from friends that lead to a page that asks users for personal contact details such as an e-mail or phone number. When users think the link was sent by a Facebook friend, they believe it is harmless and are more likely to let their guard down and share their data, becoming unwitting victims.

Sometimes simply having a social media profile can make a user a target. In 2013 Greg Boyle, a senior global–product-marketing manager for antivirus software company Trend Micro, received an e-mail notification that a person had tagged him in Facebook photos. At first, the notification appeared to be legitimate. But after closer inspection, Boyle realized that the person who supposedly tagged him was not a friend on his Facebook list, and the link did not go to Facebook photos but instead was directed to a website in Germany. After consulting with

A young woman looks through her social media sites at an Internet café. Internet thieves can find a great deal of personal information by just scrolling through people's unprotected social media pages.

security experts at Trend Micro, Boyle discovered that the e-mail was part of a Blackhole exploit kit, in which links in an e-mail direct users to another web page where malware is automatically downloaded onto their computer. This scam had been used in the past to steal banking credentials and personal information. "Luckily for me our spam filter caught the email and even if I clicked the link our web security would have blocked it," says Boyle. "For others who are not so up to date with security risks and maybe don't have the latest security protecting them, they would have fallen for what is a fairly well-crafted phishing attack."[52]

Sometimes scammers use a person's information to set up fake social media profiles, impersonating the user and targeting his or her friends with money requests or malware links. First the scammer sends a friend request to a user, who accepts the scammer into his or her Facebook circle. Once inside, the scammer has access to the user's photos, friend lists, status, and other personal information. Using this data, the scammer creates a new Facebook account posing as the user. Then the scammer starts friending the user's friends, who are unaware of the danger. The scammer then asks for money or sends messages that link to malware sites. In 2013 a woman from Raymond, New Hampshire, fell victim to

Teens at Risk

Although teens are savvy social media users, many may underestimate the danger of sharing too much personal information online. Researchers for LifeLock, an identity theft protection company, surveyed seven hundred US teens about their sharing habits in 2013. The survey found that 75 percent of teens online shared information that made themselves more vulnerable to online crime and identity theft. Many teens admitted to sharing full or partial birth dates and addresses. In addition, almost two-thirds of the teens said that they shared their school name, giving potential stalkers an easy way to find them. Even so, only about one in ten teens in the survey believed that they were too lax about protecting their identity online.

At the same time, many parents are very concerned about teens oversharing online and exposing themselves to online crime. A 2012 study by the Pew Foundation found that 53 percent of parents are very concerned that teens share too much information online. Privacy experts say that parents need to talk to teens about the dangers of oversharing online and warn them about the potential consequences. "With 75% of teenagers including some type of personal information on their social media profiles, it's clear that they don't understand the potential danger of oversharing," says Hilary Schneider, president of LifeLock. "As parents we need to engage in regular conversations with our teens about online behavior and set boundaries."

Quoted in Brian O'Connell, "Parents Are Panicked over Kids' ID Theft (Teens, Not So Much)," TheStreet, August 29, 2013. www.thestreet.com.

---

an imposter on Facebook when a scammer cloned the Facebook profile of the woman's friend. The woman was contacted by a supposed Facebook lottery agent who wanted a $600 electronic cash transfer before sending her a $70,000 lottery prize. The imposter, posing as her friend on Facebook, assured her that the lottery was legitimate. "The lottery did not make sense, but this is somebody I know and see every day of the week, so I thought it was OK,"[53] says the woman. After sending the $600, she realized too late that she had been scammed.

The creativity used by scammers on social media is increasing. Some use social media sites to post free giveaways that trick users into giving their information to a fake company or clicking a link that downloads malicious files onto a computer, putting the user at risk for identity theft. Others post viral videos that attract users. When a user clicks on the video, the file asks them to update their computer's video player. If they agree, the downloaded update is actually a virus being installed on their computer. Other scammers offer services to customize a user's social media profile. When a user accepts and installs the customization app, the scammer gains access to the user's personal data. Another common scam plays on users' natural curiosity—asking "Who viewed your profile?" When users click on the link to find out, they unknowingly download malware or are sent to malicious websites.

Online Love Scams

Online love scams prey on lonely women and men. They frequently start on Facebook, Twitter, or other social media sites. The scammer contacts the victim online, often pretending to be an American who is traveling or working abroad. They may post a picture and profile for the victim to read, which is usually fabricated or stolen from another person's website or profile. For weeks and months, the scammer and victim chat online. Eventually, the new love interest asks the victim to send money for one reason or another.

These online dating scams have become so prevalent that the FBI issued a warning about them in 2013. The warning reminded users:

> "You were targeted by criminals, probably based on personal information you uploaded on dating or social media sites."[54]
>
> —Federal Bureau of Investigation.

> You were targeted by criminals, probably based on personal information you uploaded on dating or social media sites. The pictures you were sent were most likely phony [and] lifted from other websites. The profiles were fake as well, carefully crafted to match your interests. In addition to losing your money to someone who had no intention of ever visiting you, you may also have unknowingly taken part in a money laundering scheme by cashing phony checks and sending the money overseas.[54]

In 2012 Tracy Vasseur, age forty, and her mother, Karen Vasseur, aged seventy-three, of Brighton, Colorado, were indicted for their role in an online romance scam that stole more than $1 million from 374 victims. Between 2009 and 2012 the two women worked with Nigerian associates, searching for victims on various dating and social networking sites. They established a relationship with their victims, posing as a member of the US military serving oversees. "After a phony relationship was established, victims were asked to send money and were led to believe that the soldiers would use the money to retrieve property, travel to the U.S., and pay other expenses,"[55] the Colorado attorney general's office said in a statement. The supposed military member would ask the victim to send money to an "agent" in Colorado. In one example, a man who called himself Jack Campbell told a victim to send money for travel expenses to the Vasseurs, who he claimed were military agents. In this case the victim sent ten wire transfers totaling $24,200.

Cyberbullying

Social media can be a place for people to communicate and connect with friends and family anyplace, anytime. It helps people develop and maintain friendships. It has become a fixture in daily life, changing the way people spend free time and exchange information. At the same time, however, the rise of social media has also led to a rise in cyberbullying, a form of online harassment. Using social media sites, users can embarrass, harass, or threaten others more publicly than ever before. They can post humiliating pictures or hurtful comments that hundreds of people see within minutes, adding to the victim's pain.

Across the United States, cyberbullying has become a significant problem. According to a 2013 report by the Cyberbullying Research Center, about 24 percent of high school and middle school students have been the victim of cyberbullying at some point in their lifetime. "We have seen an increase of cyberbullying," says Chief Deputy Eddie Campa of the El Paso County Sheriff's Office. "Technology is a double edge for us. It makes everything faster for us. In the past, you would write a note and pass it around; now you post something hateful online and everyone sees it. With social media and the access that kids and teenagers have to it, we have definitely seen an increase in cyberbullying."[56]

On Facebook entire pages can be used for cyberbullying. One page called 915 on Blast allows users to post stories that accuse people of various actions from bad parking to cheating on a spouse. Lorenzo Ramirez, one of the founders of 915 on Blast, defends the page and says that it was never meant to be a place for cyberbullying. "Our page 915 on Blast was created as an entertainment page; its sole purpose was meant to be a joke amongst a group of close friends. What we would do is post info about a person, nonharmful information, that only we knew," he says. Although Ramirez says that page administrators monitor the page for harmful comments, he admits they do not catch everything. "We at 915 on Blast have never condoned bullying. In a perfect world we would love to moderate every single comment as it goes live, but with so many comments coming in every second it's hard, if not near impossible,"[57] he says. Others say that pages like this condone and promote cyberbullying.

Even Olympic athletes are not immune to cyberbullying on social media. When British short track speed skater Elise Christie crashed in the 500 meter final in the 2014 Sochi Olympics, the crash also

British speed skater Elise Christie (leading the pack during a 2012 race) was subjected to online threats and harassment following a crash that took out two competitors during the 2014 Olympics. Christie dealt with the problem by cancelling her Twitter account.

Hack Attacks

No matter how diligent users are with protecting social media accounts, their privacy can be compromised by a hacker's attack on a social media site. In December 2013 hackers broke in to at least 2 million accounts and stole passwords on Facebook, Google, Twitter, Yahoo, and other sites. The hackers used key logging software that was installed on a number of computers worldwide without the owners' knowledge. The computer virus captured account sign-in information and sent user names and passwords to the hacker's server in Netherlands. Many of the social media sites notified hacked users and reset their passwords. Still, the damage had been done. The stolen information puts users and their friends at risk for identity theft and other online scams.

knocked out two other skaters. Some people were so angry over the crash they took to Twitter to harass and threaten Christie. "I've had a few people threatening me," says Christie. "Cyber-bullying basically, so it's been a tough few days. . . . I've just got to keep pushing through. I've had quite a lot of abuse over the internet to deal with, it's been tough as well. So I'm finding it quite hard."[58] After consulting with the British Olympic Association, Christie took down her Twitter account.

Real-World Threats

Allowing personal information to become public on social media sites can cost users more than money. In some cases having too much identifying information in social media posts can make users vulnerable to the real-world threats of stalkers, predators, and burglars.

According to police and child safety experts, predators are using the rising popularity of social media to victimize young people. Social media apps such as Kik, Skype, Twitter, Bendr, and Snapchat allow strangers to communicate with teens, often without their parents' knowledge. In 2013 police in Rochester, New York, began monitoring several social media sites, including one called Tagged. Police posed as a fifteen-year-old girl on the site. Almost immediately, the fake girl was approached online by a forty-three-year-old man. Within a week, he sent her sexual text messages and nude photos. The police set up a meeting with the man and then arrested him and charged him with three felonies.

In California twenty-year-old Michael Downs was sentenced in 2013 to more than fifteen years in prison after pleading no contest to molesting fifteen teenage girls that he had met on social media sites, primarily Facebook. He pretended to be sixteen years old and sent them friend requests, gaining their trust by giving the names of other teen girls and claiming to be friends with them as well. Downs eventually convinced his victims to meet him in person and then have sex with him.

The rising popularity of social media sites is also putting users at risk for stalking. "It is an old crime in a new, technological world," says Alexis Bowater, chief executive of the Network for Surviving Stalking. "The internet gives stalkers a new weapon in their armoury, a new way to find people, to follow them, to research them, sometimes to be them."[58] Bowater says that a user's digital footprint left on social networks, forums, and websites can leave clues that enable stalkers to track victims.

Social networking sites are particularly risky, as Jennifer Perry, an Internet safety expert and consumer advocate, explains:

> Almost everything shared on social networking sites can be dangerous. People put everything on Facebook: it's like a one-stop stalker shop.
>
> Photos, for example. Facebook is one of the biggest photo-sharing sites in the world, and stalkers love photos. They examine them, they manipulate them. They look at where you are, what you're doing, what you look like, how you're feeling— they will analyse every part.
>
> And then there's your friends list. Not only does the stalker stalk the victim, but (on average) they stalk 32 people around the victim. Facebook gives them a whole list of friendship connections to help them build a dynamic social map of a person. That's how powerful Facebook can be to a stalker.[60]

A New Tool for Thieves

In the past, burglars scanned newspapers for obituaries and funeral notices to target and rob grieving families. Today they turn to social media to find their victims. With Facebook, Foursquare, and Twitter, information about a person's possessions and whereabouts is often public knowledge.

With a few quick searches on social media, burglars can discover tempting targets. Then they can digitally stalk them, looking for an opportunity to strike. When users check in at a location on social media or post plans for a vacation, burglars learn when no one will be home. Google Street View allows thieves to case targets' homes from

Google Street View (pictured) is a great tool for people driving to unfamiliar locations. But it can also be used by potential thieves to get a clear picture of a house or business.

the safety of another location and plan their robbery. Facebook's location data provides a new level of information for thieves by tagging a user's post with the location where the post was made. If a thief knows where a user lives and sees a location post that shows where the user currently is, the thief knows when the user's home is empty. With this knowledge, burglars can easily target when a home and possessions are most vulnerable to theft.

A 2011 survey of convicted burglars by UK home security firm Friedland found that 78 percent said they used social media sites such as Twitter, Facebook, and Foursquare to select target properties. Fifty-four percent of the burglars said one of the most common mistakes made by homeowners was placing their status and whereabouts on social media. "We're living in the age of the digital criminal and people are taking advantage of social media to access information about would-be victims. We'll tell them even when we're going away on holidays. We will let them know that we're not in. We're inviting them round to our house,"[61] says Richard Taylor, one of the convicted burglars interviewed in the survey.

> "We're living in the age of the digital criminal and people are taking advantage of social media to access information about would-be victims."[61]
>
> —*Richard Taylor, a convicted burglar.*

In 2010 police in Nashua, New Hampshire, arrested three young men and accused them of committing approximately fifty burglaries during an August crime spree. Police investigators said the suspects used social networking sites such as Facebook to find victims who had posted online that they would not be home at a specific time. "Be careful of what you post on these social networking sites," says Ron Dickerson, a Nashua police officer. "We know for a fact that some of these players, some of these criminals, were looking on these sites and identifying their targets through these social networking sites."[62]

Staying Safe on Social Media

While social media can be used in many helpful and entertaining ways, it has also become a tool that unscrupulous criminals use to target victims, from stalking to burglary. Understanding the public nature of social networks, even when privacy settings are used, is a critical part of staying safe on social media. Cara Rousseau is the social media manager at Duke University in Durham, North Carolina, and shares information daily about the university on social media. She warns that users should always be aware that the information they post could be used against them. "It's an individual's preference for how much information he or she wants to share publicly," says Rousseau. "There's a huge range of privacy settings and ways to customize who can see your information. But the best rule of thumb is to think about anything you're putting out there as public, no matter what your privacy settings."[63]

Chapter 5

Protecting Privacy on Social Media

Launched in February 2013, Lulu is a women-only social network. After signing on to Lulu through a Facebook account, women can anonymously rate men on looks, personality, money, charm, and other categories by answering questions and using hashtags such as #MommasBoy and #IncurableRomantic. In the United States Lulu is rising in popularity, with more than 1 million users and approximately one in four college girls using the app.

In Brazil, where social media is extremely popular, Lulu quickly became the country's top downloaded app. According to the app's creator, Alexandra Chong, there were 5 million visits by girls and 300 million profiles used in Lulu's first week in Brazil. Like many of her friends, twenty-year-old Brazilian Marcela likes Lulu's concept. "I think it is cool because it's a social network for what all women throughout history have always done—talk about the guys we like, the guys we think are handsome,"[64] she says.

Some of the men being talked about on Lulu, however, have a different opinion of the social media site. Law student Felippo de Almeida Scolari says that he was upset when a friend showed him a screen shot of his Lulu profile and the hashtags girls had posted about him. He says, "I got revolted because I saw things about my intimate life exposed on the Internet for anyone to see."[65] He says that his privacy was violated because Facebook used his information for the Lulu app, something he did not authorize.

Several men who believe that Lulu violated their privacy have filed lawsuits against the company. They are also calling for legislation that will better protect privacy on social media sites. The problem, says

Internet researcher Fernando Baptista, is how to design legislation that balances a person's freedom of expression with others' right to privacy. By 2014 Lulu had revamped its app so that it will use profiles only of men who have agreed to be rated.

Who Is Responsible for Privacy?

Although users around the world have embraced social media, many are becoming increasingly concerned with the threats it poses to privacy. From online embarrassment to real-world threats, users want to be able to control who sees the information they share and decide how it is used. Their concerns are justified. According to a 2013 Pew Internet Research report titled "Anonymity, Privacy, and Security Online," 55 percent of Internet users aged eighteen to twenty-nine have experienced some difficulty when personal information has been compromised online, including having a social networking account taken over without permission, being stalked or harassed online, having personal data stolen online, suffering reputation damage, becoming a victim of an online scam, or having something happen online that put them in physical danger. For older Internet users, the dangers are slightly less but still concerning, with 42 percent of Internet users aged thirty to forty-nine experiencing a problem, along with 30 percent of those aged fifty to sixty-four and 24 percent of those ages sixty-five and older.

With a significant number of social media users experiencing privacy violations, the need to protect privacy is critical. Several parties have a role in protecting privacy online, including individual users, Internet service providers, social media sites, and the government. The majority of people (64 percent) believe that individual users have the most responsibility for protecting privacy online, according to a 2013 poll by Harris Interactive for the antivirus and security software company ESET. In comparison, only 17 percent of respondents felt Internet service providers should take responsibility for privacy online, and 12 percent felt the responsibility falls with the social media sites themselves. Additionally, only 3 percent said they thought the government and regulators bear the most responsibility for protecting privacy on social media.

Finding intimate details about one's life on a social media site can be very disconcerting. Lawmakers are trying to address the problem by crafting laws that balance free expression with the right to privacy.

Individual Privacy Measures

Individual users are often the first line of defense for privacy on social media. For some, not participating in social media is one way to ensure that their privacy is protected. According to a 2013 Pew Research Center report, about 27 percent of online adults do not participate in

Tracking Children Online

Responding to concerns about children and online privacy, the Federal Trade Commission recently updated its policies to better protect children using social media and smartphones. The new rules, which took effect in July 2013, expand the Children's Online Privacy Protection Act of 1998 (COPPA). COPPA originally mandated that website and Internet providers obtain parental consent before using, collecting, or disclosing personal information about children under age thirteen. The new rules extend to mobile devices and other technologies that did not exist in 1998 and require websites and phone apps that collect photos or geolocation data to obtain express permission from parents.

The new rules also make companies responsible for data collection by third parties on their sites. Privacy law expert Bradley Shear says that the new rules will impact social media companies and the third-party developers who create apps that target kids on social media. "I believe the updates will require Facebook to become more vigilant about policing the apps they allow on their website. The FTC has fired a warning shot to not only Facebook but to other digital ecosystems that they must do a better job of ensuring that they protect the personal privacy of children," he says.

Quoted in Bob Sullivan, "New Online Child Safety Rules Aim to Protect Kids on Social Media, Smartphones," NBC News, July 1, 2013. www.nbcnews.com.

social media platforms. They use the Internet, but not social media. In 2010 author and blogger Cory Doctorow announced that he was leaving Facebook for good, citing concerns with privacy. "By removing [myself], I thought that maybe I would in a small, incremental, personal way make Facebook slightly less enticing," he says. "I didn't want to be part of the problem."[66]

Many users who choose to use social media take steps to protect their privacy online. They are active in managing their accounts, deleting people from their friends list, deleting comments made by others on their profile, and removing their names from photos that were tagged to identify them. A majority of social network users (58 percent) restrict access to their profiles, choosing a private setting for their main profile, according to the Pew Research Internet Project. An additional 19 percent partially restrict access to their profile so that only friends and friends of friends can view it. Individuals can also protect privacy by reviewing and customizing the privacy controls on social media sites, creating adequate passwords, logging off a site after using it, and installing up-to-date antivirus- and malware-protection software.

Although users claim to value privacy, many could be doing more online to protect themselves. A 2010 study conducted by the Ponemon Institute found that although 80 percent of respondents said they were concerned about social media privacy and security, more than half acknowledged they were not taking steps to protect themselves. The researchers reported that approximately 40 percent of respondents shared their physical home address through social media, while about 65 percent admitted to not using the highest privacy settings on their social media sites. In addition, nearly 60 percent of respondents said they were unsure if their network of friends on social media were all people they could trust. "The study results are extremely telling, especially about measures that users take, or fail to take, in order to protect their identity while using social networks," says Larry Ponemon, chair and founder of the Ponemon Institute. "No matter who you are, if you want to increase social networking safety, you must take the necessary steps to protect your information."[67]

> "No matter who you are, if you want to increase social networking safety, you must take the necessary steps to protect your information."[67]
>
> —Larry Ponemon, chair and founder of the Ponemon Institute.

Social Media Sites

Social media sites have also taken steps to protect user privacy online. Sites like Facebook have designed privacy controls that allow users to customize and control the flow of information from their online profiles. Users can choose who sees what information. Most social media sites have privacy policies that explain their privacy controls, what information is collected by the site, and who sees that information. For example, Facebook's privacy policy states, "When you select an audience for your friend list, you are only controlling who can see the entire list of your friends on your timeline. We call this a timeline visibility control. This is because your friend list is always available to the games, applications, and websites you use, and your friendships may be visible elsewhere (such as on your friends' timelines or in searches)."[68] A spokesperson for the social media giant said that Facebook's privacy practices have been audited many times and found to be strong and effective. "We develop our products with 'privacy by design' in mind and to ensure our final products meet a high standard of privacy,"[69] said a Facebook representative.

Whether social media sites are doing enough to protect user privacy, however, is up for debate. In 2013 researchers from Lancaster University in the United Kingdom studied discrepancies between the privacy statements of social media sites and the sites' actual privacy controls. In their study, researchers created test accounts on several sites, including Facebook, Twitter, LinkedIn, Myspace, Bebo, and Badoo. They reviewed each site's privacy policy and compared it to its privacy controls. The researchers found that two-thirds of the principles outlined in the sites' privacy policies were not actually in place in their privacy controls. In addition, none of the sites allowed users to choose whether the site could gather information about them, prevent information from being shared with third parties, or access details on which data was shared and with whom. "Although social networking sites continue to attract millions of diverse users worldwide, they remain plagued by privacy compromises that breed user dissatisfaction and lack of trust," says coauthor Awais Rashid, a Lancaster University professor and director of Security Lancaster. "Our analysis reveals an overall lack of traceability and transparency."[70]

Since its founding in 2004, Facebook has run into trouble several times over its privacy policies. In 2007 Facebook ran a program called Beacon that allowed it to advertise to a user's friends based on their purchases on other sites. After a class-action lawsuit was settled, Facebook shut down Beacon. Then in 2009 the social network weakened user's privacy settings without telling them. In 2010 it used a program called Open Graph that gave marketers information about Facebook users' preferences. Facebook has also developed a program that takes users' information and turns it into product endorsements that are displayed on their friends' pages. In 2013 the company announced that it was removing a privacy setting that controlled whether a user's timeline could be found when people searched for them by name. "Many users are simply frustrated that the rules keep changing. Every time Facebook introduces a new feature, or unveils a new service or partnership, suddenly data is exposed in new ways that the user did not overtly consent to,"[71] says Tony Bradley, principal analyst with the Bradley Strategy Group, which provides analysis and insight on tech trends.

Ian Yip, an identity, security, and governance business manager with systems and security management company NetIQ, says that social media sites could be doing more to protect user privacy. For example, Yip says that many sites require users to change their setting to the highest privacy levels, instead of starting that way by default. "Social media sites needs to take more accountability, because privacy is a complicated thing. We've been struggling with privacy settings and privacy regulations and privacy guidelines for many, many years. For the average person, I wouldn't say it's impossible, but it's extremely difficult to understand where the boundaries are,"[72] says Yip.

In December 2013 a class-action lawsuit was filed against Facebook that accused the social network of violating the Electronic Communications Privacy Act by data mining Facebook users' private messages without permission and sharing the personal details with advertisers. Users who filed the lawsuit claimed that Facebook scanned private messages for URL links that could be used to profile users. In the suit the plaintiffs said, "Representing to users that the

> "Many users are simply frustrated that the rules keep changing. Every time Facebook introduces a new feature, or unveils a new service or partnership, suddenly data is exposed in new ways that the user did not overtly consent to."[71]
>
> —Tony Bradley, principal analyst with the Bradley Strategy Group.

content of Facebook messages is 'private' creates an especially profitable opportunity for Facebook, because users who believe they are communicating on a service free from surveillance are likely to reveal facts about themselves that they would not reveal had they known the content was being monitored."[73]

Government Regulation

Concerned that social media sites are not adequately protecting user privacy, some users are calling for the government to pass legislation that will protect privacy on social media. Currently, little federal legislation regulates privacy online. In a 2013 report from the Pew Internet & American Life Project, 68 percent of Internet users say they believe current laws are not adequate to protect their privacy.

As a result, several states have proposed a series of online-privacy laws in recent years, including ten that passed such laws in 2013 alone. "Congress is obviously not interested in updating those things or protecting privacy," says Jonathan Stickland, a Republican state representative in Texas. "If they're not going to do it, states have to do it."[74]

On January 1, 2013, California became the first state to enact comprehensive social media privacy legislation. Under the Social Media Privacy Act, universities and employers are prohibited from demanding e-mail and social media passwords. "These laws protect Californians from unwarranted invasions of their social media accounts,"[75] says California governor Jerry Brown. The California laws were passed after reports of online privacy violations nationwide and employers demanding social media passwords from job applicants. This act "is a significant step towards securing Californians' constitutional right to privacy, both online and offline,"[76]

> "Social media sites needs to take more accountability, because privacy is a complicated thing. We've been struggling with privacy settings and privacy regulations and privacy guidelines for many, many years."[72]
>
> —Ian Yip, an identity, security, and governance business manager with systems and security management company NetIQ.

says Jon Fox, consumer advocate for CALPIRG, a consumer protection group.

Several states have also passed laws that limit companies from asking employees and job applicants for access to their social media

Some companies ask employees or job candidates for user names and passwords for personal Twitter, Facebook, and other social media accounts. Several states have passed laws that limit this practice.

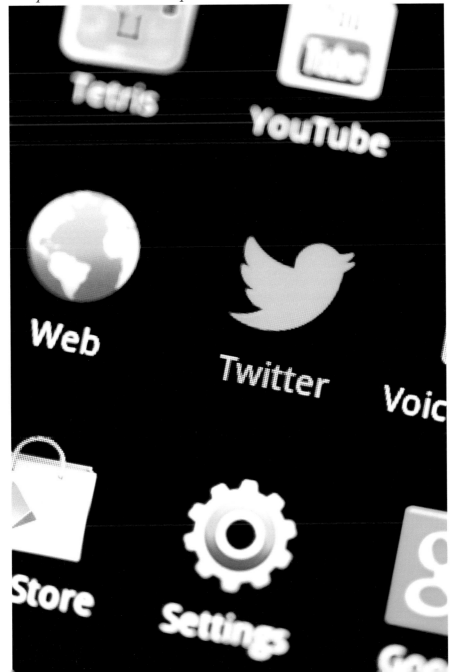

Single Sign-On

In 2010 Facebook introduced a single sign-on (SSO) mobile app that allows smartphone users to log in once to Facebook and then enter any mobile app by selecting a "Login with Facebook" button. Other companies have developed similar single sign-on tools, including Google and Twitter. Using SSO technology, users can log in once and use multiple websites without having to sign in again. The technology is popular with users, eliminating the need for multiple passwords and typing in the same information multiple times.

When used properly, SSO can make the online experience more personal for users. Jules Polonetsky, Future of Privacy Forum director, says that he uses SSO on sites like TripAdvisor or Yelp to see what his friends recommend. "[Social log-in] adds some credibility," says Polonetsky. "Last year when I was researching hotels in Paris, there were friends that had liked or been to a particular hotel, so I reached out to them. I think there's a huge value to consumers when companies respect the way the data is intended to be used. The concerns arise when companies end up being overly aggressive about sharing in ways users didn't intend."

Although convenient, SSO may put social media users at greater risk for privacy violations. SSO allows Facebook, Google, Twitter, and other sites to develop detailed user profiles that they can share with partners and advertisers, often without the user's knowledge. It also makes it easier for social media sites to show a user's actions and activities on other websites.

Quoted in Caitlin McGarry, "Don't Let Facebook's Single Sign-On Expose Your Awkward Moments," TechHive, May 31, 2013. www.techhive.com.

accounts. In May 2012 Maryland passed legislation to protect the digital privacy of employees. In July 2012 Delaware passed similar legislation to protect college students and postsecondary students from privacy invasions by their schools. In 2013 Utah passed the Internet Employment Privacy Act, which prohibits companies from asking employees for the user names and passwords of their personal accounts on Facebook, Twitter, and other social media sites. The law also prohibits employers from firing, retaliating against, or refusing to hire someone who declines to provide social media access.

Many of these state laws were enacted because of concerns that employers were becoming too aggressive in trying to access the social media accounts of applicants and employees. For example, a Michigan law was passed after an elementary school teacher's aide was fired after refusing to provide school officials access to her Facebook profile. Many other states are considering similar legislation to protect privacy rights of individuals. In Rhode Island, State Senate Majority Leader Dominick Ruggerio and State Representative Brian Kennedy introduced legislation in 2014 to limit the information employers and schools can gather from social media sites. "As more and more people use social media sites, it becomes even more important that we have laws in place to ensure their privacy and prevent outside parties—such as employers and universities—from requiring access to that personal information,"[77] says Kennedy.

> "As more and more people use social media sites, it becomes even more important that we have laws in place to ensure their privacy and prevent outside parties—such as employers and universities—from requiring access to that personal information."[77]
>
> —Brian Kennedy, a Rhode Island state representative.

Finding a Balance

The introduction of social media and the Internet has changed the way the world communicates, bringing people together from all countries, backgrounds, and ages. At the same time, the sharing of thoughts, feelings, and news on social media has triggered an increase in privacy concerns, as private information is seen and used by unintended audiences. Navigating through social media and maintaining an appropriate amount of privacy is a task for all users. Each should make his or her own choices about where the line between private and public lies, says Bradley. "When it comes to any additional information that is out there, though, users need to take some responsibility for sharing that data. Privacy and social networking are at opposite ends of the spectrum and it's up to the individual user to exercise discretion in sharing information, and utilize the controls provided to place the fulcrum in the right spot to find a balance between the two that is comfortable,"[78] he says.

Source Notes

Introduction: Unintended Consequences

1. Quoted in ESPN.com, "Recruit Yuri Wright Expelled for Tweets," January 20, 2012. http://espn.go.com.
2. Quoted in ESPN.com, "Recruit Yuri Wright Expelled for Tweets."
3. Quoted in Andy Staples, "For Top Football Recruits, Behavior on Social Media Has Consequences," *Sports Illustrated*, January 24, 2012. http://sportsillustrated.cnn.com.
4. Quoted in Staples, "For Top Football Recruits, Behavior on Social Media Has Consequences."

Chapter 1: The History of Privacy and Social Media

5. Frederick S. Lane, *American Privacy: The 400-Year History of Our Most Contested Right*. Boston: Beacon, 2009.
6. *Amendment IV: Search and Seizure*, US Constitution, National Constitution Center. http://constitutioncenter.org.
7. Quoted in Anne Flaherty, "Study Finds Online Privacy Concerns on the Rise," Yahoo News, September 5, 2013. http://news.yahoo.com.
8. Lane, *American Privacy*.
9. Quoted in Geoffrey Fowler, "When the Most Personal Secrets Get Outed on Facebook," *Wall Street Journal*, October 13, 2012. http://online.wsj.com.
10. Quoted in Beth Greenfield, "Blogger Unwittingly Becomes Diet Poster Girl. Now She's Fighting Back," Yahoo Shine, March 12, 2013. http://shine.yahoo.com.
11. Quoted in Greenfield, "Blogger Unwittingly Becomes Diet Poster Girl. Now She's Fighting Back."
12. Quoted in Bob Sullivan, "Why Should I Care About Digital Privacy?," NBC News, March 11, 2011. www.nbcnews.com.

13. Quoted in Sullivan, "Why Should I Care About Digital Privacy?"
14. Quoted in Adam Tanner, "Users More Savvy About Social Media Privacy than Thought, Poll Finds," *Forbes*, November 13, 2013. www.forbes.com.
15. Quoted in Nathan Eddy, "Social Media Users Fail to Protect Their Privacy: ESET," eWeek, November 14, 2013. www.eweek.com.
16. Bruce Schneier, "Google and Facebook's Privacy Illusion," *Forbes*, April 6, 2010. www.forbes.com.
17. Quoted in Fowler, "When the Most Personal Secrets Get Outed on Facebook."
18. Quoted in Fowler, "When the Most Personal Secrets Get Outed on Facebook."
19. Quoted in Fowler, "When the Most Personal Secrets Get Outed on Facebook."
20. danah boyd, "Making Sense of Privacy and Publicity," SXSW, March 13, 2010. www.danah.org.

Chapter 2: Sharing Information Online

21. Quoted in Matt Pierce, "NPR Host Scott Simon Tweets His Mother's Dying Days," *Los Angeles Times*, July 30, 2013. www.latimes.com.
22. Quoted in *New York Times* Customer Insight Group, "The Psychology of Sharing: Why Do People Share Online?," SlideShare, 2011. www.slideshare.net.
23. Quoted in Elizabeth Blair, "Online, Researcher Says, Teens Do What They've Always Done," NPR, February 25, 2014. www.npr.org.
24. Quoted in Mary Madden, "Teens, Social Media, and Privacy," Pew Research Internet Project, May 21, 2013. www.pewinternet.org.
25. Quoted in *New York Times* Customer Insight Group, "The Psychology of Sharing."
26. Quoted in *New York Times* Customer Insight Group, "The Psychology of Sharing."
27. Quoted in Bob Sullivan, "Study: Social Media Polarizes Our Privacy Concerns," NBC News, March 10, 2011. www.nbcnews.com.

28. Quoted in Holly Ellyatt, "Users Quitting Facebook Cite Privacy Concerns," *Daily Beast*, September 19, 2013. www.thedailybeast .com.

29. Quoted in Byron Acohido, "Facebook Tracking Is Under Scrutiny," *USA Today*, November 16, 2011. http://usatoday30.usatoday .com.

30. Quoted in Sharon Jayson, "Social Media Research Raises Privacy and Ethics Issues," *USA Today*, March 12, 2014. www.usatoday .com.

31. Quoted in Jayson, "Social Media Research Raises Privacy and Ethics Issues."

Chapter 3: Public Versus Private Lives

32. Quoted in Elise Sole, "Daughter's Facebook Brag Costs Her Family $80,000," Yahoo Shine, February 28, 2014. http://shine .yahoo.com.

33. Quoted in Sole, "Daughter's Facebook Brag Costs Her Family $80,000."

34. Quoted in Aly Thomson, "Saint Mary's University Under Cloud of Controversy Again, This Time over Tweets," Yahoo Sports, January 28, 2014. http://ca.sports.yahoo.com.

35. Quoted in Greg Beaubien, "Weiner Scandal Is Latest Reminder of Power, Perils of Social Media," *Public Relations Strategist*, Summer 2011. https://prsa.org.

36. Quoted in Brian Stelter, "'Ashamed': Ex-PR Exec Justine Sacco Apologizes for AIDS in Africa Tweet," CNN, December 22, 2013. www.cnn.com.

37. Quoted in Stelter, "'Ashamed.'"

38. Quoted in Natasha Singer, "They Loved Your G.P.A. Then They Saw Your Tweets," *New York Times*, November 9, 2013. www.ny times.com.

39. Quoted in Singer, "They Loved Your G.P.A. Then They Saw Your Tweets."

40. Quoted in Singer, "They Loved Your G.P.A. Then They Saw Your Tweets."

41. Quoted in Singer, "They Loved Your G.P.A. Then They Saw Your Tweets."

42. Quoted in Dara Kerr, "Facebookers, Beware: That Silly Update Can Cost You a Job," CNET, May 29, 2013. http://news.cnet .com.
43. Quoted in CBS News, "Did the Internet Kill Privacy?," February 6, 2011. www.cbsnews.com.
44. Quoted in CBS News, "Did the Internet Kill Privacy?"
45. Quoted in Erik Lacitis, "Bitter Barista Loses Job over Snarky Blog About Customers, Boss," *Seattle Times*, February 11, 2013. http://seattletimes.com.
46. Quoted in Lacitis, "Bitter Barista Loses Job over Snarky Blog About Customers, Boss."
47. Quoted in Casey Wian, "Friend: Hannah Anderson Discusses Kidnapping on Social Media," CNN, August 15, 2013. www.cnn .com.
48. Quoted in ABC 10News, "Controversial New Book Written About Hannah Anderson Kidnapping Case," October 7, 2013. www.10news.com.

Chapter 4: Scams and Threats

49. Quoted in Jason Knowles, "Social Media Scam Targets Facebook, Twitter, Instagram Users' Relatives," ABC News, February 14, 2014. http://abclocal.go.com.
50. Quoted in Knowles, "Social Media Scam Targets Facebook, Twitter, Instagram Users' Relatives."
51. Quoted in Jam Kotenko, "Facebook Identity Fraud Is Up and You Need to Be Careful," Digital Trends, August 30, 2013. www.digi taltrends.com.
52. Greg Boyle, "It Pays to Know Who Your Friends Are," Trend Micro, August 20, 2013. http://blog.trendmicro.com.
53. Quoted in Mark Hayward, "Woman Falls Victim to Facebook Profile 'Cloning' Scam," *Manchester New Hampshire Union Leader*, December 22, 2013. www.unionleader.com.
54. Darrell Foxworth, "Looking for Love? Beware of Online Dating Scams," FBI: San Diego Division, February 14, 2013. www.fbi.gov.
55. Quoted in Susanna Kim, "Colorado Mother and Daughter Charged in Online Dating Scam with Fake Military Members," ABC News, June 25, 2012. http://abcnews.go.com.

56. Quoted in Aaron Martinez, "Cyberbullying: El Paso Girl's Suicide Puts Spotlight on Social Media Dangers," *El Paso Times* (Texas), January 12, 2014. www.elpasotimes.com.

57. Quoted in Martinez, "Cyberbullying."

58. Quoted in Paul Jones, "Sochi 2014: Hazel Irvine Slams Cyber-Bullies as Team GB Skater Elise Christie Is Disqualified Again," RadioTimes, February 15, 2014. www.radiotimes.com.

59. Quoted in Alexandra Topping, "Social Networking Sites Fuelling Stalking, Report Warns," *Manchester (UK) Guardian*, February 1, 2012. www.theguardian.com.

60. Quoted in Harriet Lawrence, "How Can I Stay Safe Online?," Digital Stalking, December 3, 2012. www.digital-stalking.com.

61. Quoted in Shea Bennett, "4 Out of 5 Burglars Use Twitter and Facebook to Select Victims, Says Survey," Mediabistro, September 27, 2011. www.mediabistro.com.

62. Quoted in WMUR, "Police: Thieves Robbed Homes Based on Facebook, Social Media Sites," September 13, 2010. www.wmur.com.

63. Quoted in Cara Bonnett, "Staying Safe on Social Network Sites," Duke Today, October 5, 2011. https://today.duke.edu.

Chapter 5: Protecting Privacy on Social Media

64. Quoted in Lourdes Garcia-Navarro, "Brazil's Social Media Boom Sparks Calls for New Privacy Laws," NPR, January 1, 2014. www.npr.org.

65. Quoted in Garcia-Navarro, "Brazil's Social Media Boom Sparks Calls for New Privacy Laws."

66. Quoted in Ki Mae Heussner, "Tech Biggies Quit Facebook over Privacy Flap: Will Others Follow?," ABC News, May 14, 2010. http://abcnews.go.com.

67. Quoted in ProtectMyID, "News Release: The Truth About Social Media Identity Theft; Perception Versus Reality," Experian, June 21, 2010. www.protectmyid.com.

68. Facebook, "Data Use Policy," March 12, 2014. www.facebook.com.

69. Quoted in Michael Lee, "Is Privacy Too Complex for Social Media to Handle Alone?," ZDNet, January 13, 2014 www.zdnet.com.

70. Quoted in Phys.org, "Social Media Plagued by Privacy Problems, Say Researchers," May 21, 2013. http://phys.org.

71. Tony Bradley, "Facebook Privacy: Mea Culpa Reality Check," *PC World*, May 15, 2010. www.pcworld.com.

72. Quoted in Lee, "Is Privacy Too Complex for Social Media to Handle Alone?"

73. Quoted in Christine Zibas, "Class Action Lawsuit Against Facebook Contends Company Violates Users' Privacy," Legal Source 360, January 5, 2014. www.legalsource360.com.

74. Quoted in Somini Sengupta, "No U.S. Action, So States Move on Privacy Law," *New York Times*, October 30, 2013. www.nytimes.com.

75. Quoted in Dina Abou, "California First to Endorse Comprehensive Social Media Privacy Law," *Nation* (blog), ABC News, December 27, 2012. http://abcnews.go.com.

76. Quoted in Abou, "California First to Endorse Comprehensive Social Media Privacy Law."

77. Quoted in Alek Matthiessen, "R.I. Politicians Propose Social Media Privacy Legislation," *Brown Daily Herald* (Brown University, Providence, RI), February 20, 2013. www.browndailyherald.com.

78. Bradley, "Facebook Privacy."

Online Privacy Tips

Basic Security

- Use security software to block viruses and malware. Keep it up to date.
- Use passwords at least eight characters long. Add numerals and punctuation to make them harder to guess.
- Back up important data to a flash or USB drive or an online service.

E-mail and Messaging

- Do not click on web links or attachments in e-mail or text messages unless you are expecting them. (Strange messages from a friend may indicate that their account has been "hijacked.")
- Beware of "scary" messages that claim to be from a bank or government agency. Contact the agency directly if you think there might be a problem.
- Do not put credit card numbers or other sensitive information in e-mail or text messages.

Web and Social Networks

- Learn about browser features that can enhance security and privacy.
- Find and use the privacy settings for Facebook, Twitter, and other social networks.
- Do not post personal details or other information that you wouldn't want a stranger to know.

Banking and E-Commerce

- Make payments only on secure web pages (indicated by https:// in the address and a padlock symbol).

- Do not do banking or online purchases on a public Wifi network.
- Monitor bank and credit card accounts regularly for signs of fraud.

Mobile Devices

- Protect your phone or tablet with a passcode.
- Install software that allows you to track or disable lost or stolen devices.
- Install apps from only trusted sources.
- Check settings to see what information apps may be obtaining from your device.

Finally . . .

- Think before you hit "Send." You cannot take your words back.
- Common sense and courtesy can go a long way.

Related Organizations and Websites

American Civil Liberties Union (ACLU)

125 Broad St., 18th Floor
New York, NY 10004
phone: (212) 549-2500
website: www.aclu.org

The ACLU works daily in courts, legislatures, and communities to defend and preserve the rights—including the right to privacy—and liberties of everyone in the United States.

Electronic Frontier Foundation (EFF)

815 Eddy St.
San Francisco, CA 94109
phone: (415) 436-9333
fax: (415) 436-9993
e-mail: info@eff.org
website: www.eff.org

Founded in 1990, the EFF is a nonprofit organization dedicated to defending consumer rights in a digital world.

Electronic Privacy Information Center (EPIC)

1718 Connecticut Ave. NW, Suite 200
Washington, DC 20009
phone: (202) 483-1140
fax: (202) 483-1248
website: www.epic.org

EPIC is a public interest research center in Washington, DC, that strives to focus public attention on emerging civil liberties issues and to protect privacy, the First Amendment, and constitutional values. EPIC publishes an e-mail and online newsletter on civil liberties in the information age, along with reports and books on other topics related to civil liberties.

Federal Trade Commission (FTC)

600 Pennsylvania Ave. NW
Washington, DC 20580
phone: (202) 326-2222
website: www.ftc.gov

The FTC is a federal government organization that is actively involved with privacy concerns of consumers, including Internet privacy. The FTC website aims to educate users about laws and privacy initiatives.

Identity Theft Resource Center (ITRC)

9672 Via Excelencia
San Diego, CA 92126
phone: (858) 693-7935
e-mail: itrc@idtheftcenter.org
website: www.idtheftcenter.org

The ITRC is a nonprofit organization dedicated to the understanding and prevention of identity theft. The ITRC provides victim and consumer support and public education. It also advises governmental agencies, legislators, law enforcement, and businesses about the evolving and growing problem of identity theft.

Pew Research Center's Internet & American Life Project

1615 L St. NW, Suite 700
Washington, DC 20036
phone: (202) 419-4500

fax: (202) 419-4505
website: www.pewinternet.org

The Pew Research Center's Internet & American Life Project is one of seven projects that make up the Pew Research Center, a nonpartisan, nonprofit fact tank that provides information on the issues, attitudes, and trends shaping America and the world. The project studies the Internet and digital technologies shaping the world today.

Ponemon Institute

2308 US 31 N.
Traverse City, MI 49686
phone: (231) 938-9900
fax: (231) 938-6215
website: www.ponemon.org

The Ponemon Institute conducts independent research on privacy, data protection, and information security policy.

Privacy Rights Clearinghouse (PRC)

3108 Fifth Ave., Suite A
San Diego, CA 92103
phone: (619) 298-3396
website: www.privacyrights.org

The PRC is a nonprofit organization that engages, educates, and empowers individuals to protect their privacy. It has a complaint center to report privacy abuses, as well as fact sheets, articles, and other information about online privacy issues.

For Further Research

Books

Cynthia A. Bily, *The Internet*. Farmington Hills, MI: Greenhaven, 2012.

danah boyd, *It's Complicated: The Social Lives of Networked Teens*. New Haven, CT: Yale University Press, 2014.

Ted Claypoole and Theresa Payton, *Protecting Your Internet Identity: Are You Naked Online?* Lanham, MD: Rowman & Littlefield, 2012.

Stephen Currie, *Online Privacy*. San Diego, CA: ReferencePoint, 2011.

Stephen Currie, *How Is the Internet Eroding Privacy Rights?* San Diego, CA: ReferencePoint, 2014.

Corey Sandler, *Living with the Internet and Online Dangers*. New York: Facts On File, 2010.

Suzanne Weinick, *Understanding Your Rights in the Information Age*. New York: Rosen, 2013.

Internet Sources

Pew Research Center's Internet & American Life Project, "Teens, Social Media, and Privacy," May 21, 2013. www.pewinternet.org /2013/05/21/teens-social-media-and-privacy.

Pew Research Center's Internet & American Life Project, "Anonymity, Privacy, and Security Online," September 5, 2013. www.pewinter net.org/2013/09/05/anonymity-privacy-and-security-online.

Websites

AnnualCreditReport.com (www.annualcreditreport.com). Users who suspect they may be victims of identity theft may order free annual credit reports at this website.

GetNetWise (www.getnetwise.org). Information and tutorials about the latest issues and concerns facing Internet users, including safety, wireless security, and spyware.

NetSmartz (www.netsmartz.org). From the National Center for Missing and Exploited Children, this site has information about topics that relate to privacy and social media, including cyberbullying, revealing too much information, social networking, and more.

OnGuard Online (www.onguardonline.gov). This site provides practical tips from the federal government and the technology industry to help users be on guard against Internet fraud, secure their computers, and protect their personal information.

Online Privacy (http://oag.ca.gov/privacy/online-privacy). This site from the State of California Department of Justice has links to resources and fact sheets about staying safe and protecting privacy online.

Privacy.org (www.privacy.org). This site offers the latest news, information, and initiatives on privacy. It is a joint project of the Electronic Privacy Information Center and Privacy International.

StaySafeOnline (www.staysafeonline.org). From the National Cyber Security Alliance, this site offers information and tools to help people use the Internet safely and securely at home, work, and school.

Index

Quinn, Sarah, 37

Rains, J.P., 30–31
Ramirez, Lorenzo, 47
relationships, 10, 22–23
reputations damaged, 4, 30–32, **31**, 33
research using digital footprints, 27
Rhode Island, 63
robbery, **50**, 50–51
Ross, Gary L., 34
Rousseau, Cara, 52
Ruggerio, Dominick, 63

scams
    automatic downloading of malware, 42–43, 45
    free giveaways, 45
    requesting money, 41, 43–44, 46
    romance, 45–46
Schneider, Hilary, 44
Schneier, Bruce, 15
school and college officials
    monitoring of students' accounts, 36
    permanence of postings and, 32
    state privacy laws and, 62, 63
    use during admissions process, 4, 33–35
Scolari, Felippo de Almeida, 53
screen shots of chats, 11–12
security
    parties responsible for, 15, 33, 54, 56
    percent of users concerned about, 57
    percent of users not taking precautions, 57
    by teenagers protecting identity, 44
    user measures, 56–57
    users not sure about network of friends, 57
self-confidence factor, 10
self-esteem factor, 23
self-fulfillment factor, 23
service providers' responsibility for security, 54
Shear, Bradley, 29, 56
Simon, Scott, 18
single sign-on (SSO) mobile, 62
smartphones, 16, 62
Snay, Dana, 29
Snay, Patrick, 29
snooping, 13
Social Media Privacy Act (California), 60–61
social media sites
    about, 11
    percent of adults not on, 55–56
    positive aspects of, 10
    as public forums, 29
    as responsible for security, 54, 56, 59
    use of multiple sites, 19
SSO (single sign-on) mobile, 62
stalking, 49
state laws, 60–63
Stickland, Jonathan, 60
Stieger, Stefan, 25
Supreme Court decisions, 7–8

tablets, 16
Tansley, Rhys, 30
targeted advertising, 27
Taylor, Richard, 51
teenagers
    cyberbullying of, 46

dangers of communicating with strangers, 48–49
importance of fame to, 22
opinions about effect of social media on relationships,
    10
use by
    frequency of, 20
    increase in sharing of personal information, 21
    percent, 20
    sites, 20–21
    vulnerability to online crime and identity theft, 44
theft, **50**, 50–51
Toal, Greg, 4
tracking activity, 25–27, 51, 62
Trend Micro, 19, 42–43
Twitter users
    account password thefts, 48
    followers and, 18
    number of (2013), 11
    school and college officials, 4, 33
    teenagers, 20, 21
    time spent on mobile devices compared to computers,
        16
    time spent on weekly, 11

Uhls, Yalda, 22
users
    effect on relationships of, 10
    followers and, 18
    hiding online activity by, 8
    number of, 11, 42
    percent experiencing problems with compromised
        personal information, 54
    privacy policies/controls of sites and, 26
        choices, 57–58
        confusion about, 14, 24–25
        use of, 56–57
    privacy settings to control information, 13
    quitting due to privacy concerns, 24–25
    as responsible for security, 15, 33, 54
    time spent by, 11, 16
    tracking online activity by, 26
    worry about availability of online information, 8
    See also teenagers
Utah, 62–63

Varsity Monitor, 36
Vasseur, Karen, 46
Vasseur, Tracy, 46
videos, going viral, 45
Vine, 18
viral videos, 45
Voth, Bill, 36

Wages, Preston, 5–6
Walsh, Wendy, 39
warrants, obtaining, 7
Watson, Matt, 38
Web 2.0, 10–11
Weiner, Anthony, 31, 31–32
Wiseman, Kieran, 33
World Wide Web, 9–11
Wright, Yuri, 4

Yahoo, account password thefts, 48
Yip, Ian, 59
YouTube, 11, 22

80